In *Preaching That Moves People*, ⸻⸻⸻ shares actionable
wisdom to help you preach your best sermon. I have benefited greatly
from Yancey's preaching and he does phenomenal work developing other
preachers. You can trust him to help you, and you'll want to
share this book with a friend.

MATT ADAIR
Lead Pastor, Christ Community Church, Athens, GA
Founder of the *Your Best Sermon* preaching system

There are a ton of books on preaching out there, but most of them deal
primarily with how to prepare and write a sermon. Yancey has written a
book that is unique in that it clearly walks through the actual delivery of the
sermon — how are you going to say it to your people in a way that moves
them? This is a great resource for anyone who preaches or aspires to preach.
I highly recommend it!

MATT CARTER
Pastor of Preaching and Vision, Austin Stone Community Church, Austin, TX
Author of *Steal Away Home*

I've had the opportunity to sit under the Yancey's preaching on many
occasions. He is a man used by God in edifying and encouraging ways as
he preaches. This book isn't a book of pragmatics but wisdom
wrung from experience and the disciplined pursuit of God.

MATT CHANDLER
Lead Teaching Pastor, The Village Church, Dallas, TX
Author of *The Explicit Gospel*

The best preachers love the process as well as the content of
communication. Yancey Arrington is one of those, as is well demonstrated
in this helpful book on the effective delivery and pace of a sermon that
takes into account the "necessities and capacities" of modern listeners.

BRYAN CHAPELL
Senior Pastor, Grace Presbyterian Church, Peoria, IL
President Emeritus of Knox Theological Seminary
Author of *Christ-Centered Preaching*

There are few things more excruciating than listening to a boring sermon, and preaching a boring sermon is at the top of the list. In *Preaching That Moves People*, avid skier and engaging preacher Yancey Arrington finds the solution to snoring congregations at the intersection of his two great passions. This book is both accessible for young preachers who are just finding their voice and insightful for experienced preachers from any theological tradition. I found myself applying what I read in the very next sermon I preached. I am going to hand this book to every wannabe preacher in my church (and all the crusty old preachers, too).

NOEL JESSE HEIKKINEN
Lead Pastor, Riverview Church, Holt, MI
Author of *Unchained: If Jesus Has Set Us Free, Why Don't We Feel Free?*

Faithful preaching not only informs the mind, but also moves the heart. It does more than change the way we think, it transforms the very core of who we are. In *Preaching That Moves People*, Yancey has given preachers of all levels of experience a great gift drawn from his own immense experience. This book will encourage you, equip you, and help you engage new practices in your preaching ministry.

RYAN HUGULEY
Lead Pastor, Ridgeline Church, Salt Lake City, UT
Author of *8 Hours or Less: Writing Faithful Sermons Faster*

Learning to craft a sermon is the preacher's life-long endeavor. *Preaching That Moves People* is a brilliant, practical, and informative tool that will advance us in this endeavor. My friend Yancey Arrington has given us a framework to de-clutter and clear confusion from our sermons as we seek to more clearly communicate God's Word. All preachers, in every context, should read this book.

DOUG LOGAN
Lead Pastor, Epiphany Fellowship, Camden, NJ
Author of *On the Block*

We need more resources on effective sermon delivery, especially from those that have a conviction about Christ-centered expository preaching. And here's one! Yancey speaks as a scholar (aware of the discussions on preaching) and as a practitioner (engaged in the regular grind of pastoral preaching). As I read *Preaching that Moves People*, I reflected on several conversations that I've had recently with young pastors. Several have talked to me about how their preaching can come across as dry and academic. How can they fix this? They don't want to sacrifice their commitment to substantive exposition. Yancey shows us how to avoid this problem – how we can be both engaging and thoroughly biblical. I wholeheartedly recommend it!

TONY MERIDA
Pastor for Preaching and Vision, Imago Dei Church, Raleigh, NC
Former Associate Professor of Preaching at Southeastern Seminary
Author of *The Christ-Centered Expositor*

In an age where Christians pursue life in Christ outside the local church more than ever before, there has been perhaps no more important time to recover the art of preaching Scripture-drenched, Christ-centered, community-forming, and neighbor-loving sermons. Among the many books written to help preachers refine this skill, Yancey has written one of the better ones. I highly recommend *Preaching that Moves People* to all current and aspiring preachers. I trust that as you work through this volume, you too will be moved.

SCOTT SAULS
Senior Pastor, Christ Presbyterian Church, Nashville, TN
Author of *From Weakness to Strength*

Yancey Arrington is passionate about gospel-centered and people-centered preaching. From his 30-year journey, he reminds us that communicating to impact people at a heart level requires theologically sound doctrine and emotionally sound delivery. In other words, both the message and the messenger matter! *Preaching That Moves People* is a proven field manual that is a must read for preaching pastors.

BILL WELLONS
Founding Pastor, Fellowship Bible Church, Little Rock, AR
Director, Fellowship Associates Church Planting Leadership Residency

PREACHING THAT MOVES PEOPLE

How to get down the mountain of
your messages with maximum impact

YANCEY ARRINGTON

CLEAR CREEK  RESOURCES

Preaching That Moves People:
How to Get Down the Mountain of Your Messages
with Maximum Impact

Copyright © 2018 by Yancey C. Arrington
Published by Clear Creek Resources

999 N. Egret Bay Blvd.
League City, Texas 77573

ISBN 978-0-9979469-0-1

Unless otherwise indicated, all Scripture quotations are taken from:

The ESV® Bible (The Holy Bible, English Standard Version®), copyright © 2001 by Crossway, a publishing ministry of Good News Publishers. Used by permission. All rights reserved.

All Scripture emphases have been added by the author.

First printing, 2018.

Printed in the United States of America

To the people of Clear Creek Community Church,
its preaching cohort,
and my pastor-friends from parts far and wide
who consistently encouraged me to put in book-form
what I've thought and taught about preaching over the years.

CONTENTS

ACKNOWLEDGMENTS

This year completes my twentieth of pulpit ministry as the Teaching Pastor of Clear Creek Community Church. I would not be the preacher I am today if it weren't for the patience and guidance of Dr. Bruce Wesley and the rest of our leadership staff (not to mention our congregation). Bruce persistently encouraged me to write down how I think about preaching, and this book is the result: the fruit of my thoughts about preaching in order to train CCCC's preaching cohort. Bruce's kind prodding to write this book has been a blessing in itself.

Heartfelt thanks also go to Jeff Lawrence, one of my closest friends and also a wonderful thinker, writer, and pastor. He was kind enough to read my first draft and offer insights that re-shaped the book. I am incredibly grateful for his contribution to this endeavor, but more so for his friendship.

This is the second book on which Mandy Turner has served as my editor. Add Mandy's literary acumen on top of her intelligence in fields both grammatical and theological, and you have a boon for an author like me. My mantra for her with this project was the same as my last: turn a speaker into a writer. She has done exactly that (though I'm confident it has taken much work). There is rarely a paragraph that has escaped her deft touch, and for that I am deeply appreciative.

A quick thanks to Jon Coffey, Ryan Lehtinen, Daniel Palacios, and Mason Cheatham for proofing my manuscript.

I want to express my gratitude for the pulpit ministries of John MacArthur, Tommy Nelson, John Piper, and Timothy Keller. These men have been formative influences in my preaching over the years. You will read in this book how they specifically impacted my ministry, but I would be remiss if I did not acknowledge them here.

In that same spirit, I want to express my appreciation for Bryan Chapell. I had the pleasure of taking Bryan's class on Christ-centered preaching during my doctoral studies at Covenant Seminary. I was so taken by his approach to redemptive-oriented preaching that I asked permission to use some of his material for my preaching seminars. To this day, in all my endeavors to train preachers, Bryan's *Christ-Centered Preaching* is the one resource I recommend more than any. Frankly, it's knowing we have stellar books on preaching such as his, that frees me to write one like mine.

I'm deeply grateful for my Acts 29 family, whose national conference provided the first opportunity for a large group presentation of my perspective on preaching. The encouragement I received from fellow pastors there was one of the chief drivers for me to start this book as soon as possible. There are few greater joys than hearing from other preachers about how their pulpits have been positively impacted by the ideas within *Preaching That Moves People*.

Finally, I want to thank my wife, Jennefer, for her continual love and support. She, like Bruce, patiently and persistently kept my feet to the fire about writing this book. Jennefer would regularly ask, "So, when are you going to start your preaching book?" with the expectation of a timeline or, at least, a start date. My assumption is in a few years, that question will surface again for my next project. Thanks for pushing me, Jen; I love you.

FOREWORD

*I*f *you can't hire the best, hire the one who will become the best.* I think John Maxwell said it, but I repeated it to the elders of our four-year-old church plant. While preaching is one of my gifts, it's not my first gift, so we were seeking to add a gifted preacher to our pastoral staff. The elders saw Yancey Arrington's raw giftedness, sharp mind, strong theological conviction, and bold personality, and we believed Yancey would become one of the best preachers anywhere. We were right.

For twenty years, I have enjoyed a front-row seat in Yancey's life as God has transformed a good preacher into a great preacher. But more importantly, I have walked closely enough to see Yancey live as a disciple of Jesus. I am inspired by his deep conviction in the power of the gospel, the sufficiency of Scripture, and the wonder of the local church. I have watched Yancey love his family, be a good friend, and serve as a faithful pastor.

Yancey is my partner in the teaching ministry of the church. He's also one of the primary influencers in my preaching. Over the years, I noticed that Yancey's preaching felt more like an experience than a lecture. When he preached, people were lost in the moment. They were going somewhere with him. Consistently, people were moved. They were moved emotionally, they were moved to believe, and they were moved to change.

So, one day, I asked Yancey some questions about how he

thinks about preaching. I wanted to learn how to take people somewhere when I preached too. To my surprise, he didn't know how to help me. He had never thought about it. Like many people with extreme gifting, Yancey could write and preach messages that were both engaging and impactful, but he couldn't tell someone else how to do it.

I urged Yancey to think about how to help other preachers do what came so naturally to him. And he did. Now you hold in your hands a treasure for everyone who preaches the gospel. The concepts in this book are the result of years of Yancey's devotion to help others think about preaching in a way that moves people.

The content of this book has been tested as Yancey trained the preaching cohort at Clear Creek Community Church. As a result, our preaching got better. We use the language in this book in our everyday conversations about shaping and evaluating sermons. Yancey has also provided training for church planters and pastors in workshops for the Houston Church Planting Network and others across the country. Experienced pastors like me, who have preached for years, have urged Yancey to write this book because the ideas herein have been so helpful.

I believe this book is a unique contribution to the preaching genre. In 35 years of preaching, I have not seen a single book that addresses the vital topics that Yancey unpacks here, like arranging for tension, building for speed, and considering the emotional flow of the message. These ideas did not reshape my theology. I did not change the content of my messages. Rather, through applying what Yancey addresses here, I simply became a better preacher. And that's a gift, not only to me, but to everyone who hears me preach.

So, I hope you will read with a pen in your hand. It's a quick read, but it might take you some time to learn to effectively apply the powerful concepts. Even if this way of thinking about messages does not come naturally to you in the beginning, it will be worth the effort. You will grow in your ability to take people on a life-changing journey of following Jesus. Your preaching will move people.

Dr. Bruce Wesley

Founding and Senior Pastor, Clear Creek Community Church, Houston
founder, Houston Church Planting Network

INTRODUCTION

The primary task of the Church and of the Christian minister is the preaching of the Word of God.

– MARTYN LLOYD-JONES, *PREACHING AND PREACHERS*

All of us who have preached for any number of years remember times when we left the pulpit pleased with our sermon. Surely you know the feeling. The congregation appears to be "locked in". Men and women lean forward, engaged with every movement of your message. You feel as if you are in the zone: every point, every illustration, every nuance within the sermon seems to be finding its target with your congregants. You're connecting! There's a life in the pulpit so tangible you can feel it. All the words pouring from your mouth feel less like a sermon delivered from your head and more like a message flowing from your heart. You can sense that this is a moment when you help people hear from God in a way that makes a significant impact on their spiritual formation. All the while your spouse proudly beams at you from her spot in the sanctuary with a smile that says, "That's the preacher I knew he could be!"

These are the sacred moments that make us so incredibly grateful to God for the opportunity to preach in a local church. It's like a golfer hitting the perfect shot. He's so excited about his near-perfect execution that his glee covers his recent tally of mis-hits, duffs, and shanks, when his golf game had been more akin to ditch-digger than sportsman. Indeed, his wonder shot produces such great encouragement that he says to himself, "Man, I love this game! I can't wait for my next tee time." I'm confident you have preached a wonder-shot sermon a time or two. You leave the pulpit with such an incredible feeling of joy that you can't wait to return next week.

Then there are times that are quite the opposite. Somewhat ironically, it often happens on the immediate Sunday after you crushed it in the pulpit. Now the sermon feels like preaching in quicksand, with no traction for your hearers whatsoever. The dynamic of the room is at a low ebb – if not completely dead. You walk away beating yourself up and wondering where it all went wrong. You can't bear to look at your spouse, much less ask her what she thought of that abject failure you call your sermon. Even worse is finding yourself marooned in an entire season of preaching these kinds of messages. It can be so discouraging that you question if you are called to preach at all.

You wonder what went wrong. What eats at you is that you didn't prepare differently or throw something together the night before. If you could compare the week of sermon prep for your *I-can't-believe-I-get-to-preach* sermon with the week of prep for your *I-can't-believe-I-still-have-a-job* message, there is no discernible difference. Yet there's also no question the second preaching experience was the emotional equivalent of driving the ball into the woods, into a sand trap, killing a bird in flight, into another sand trap, hitting your golf buddy, then mercifully picking up the ball to save yourself from further embarrassment. At this point you're just praying to finish the rest of the course by dusk and retire for the evening – if not from the game of golf for good.

The first question that surfaces in the wake of a bad sermon is simply, "Why?" *Why was this preaching event so terrible? Why did it seem the people were so distant? Why did I feel like I was preaching in quicksand? Why did one sermon seem to connect and move my congregants, while the other did exactly the opposite?*

Why? Why? Why? Listen, keep your chin up. Take heart. Don't throw your clubs in the trash. You are not the only one to feel that way. I would venture most every preacher worth his salt has experienced those disastrous days in the pulpit and the anxiety, fear, and depression that come with them. I know I sure have.

THE 'HOW' MATTERS

In my years of preaching and training other preachers, I have frequently found that the common root of our mis-hit messages is sermon delivery. Multitudes of preachers are adept at finding a biblical text, studying that text, and preparing messages based on that text. Their work clearly displays competency in sermon composition. Unfortunately, their effort is accompanied by a woeful lack of thought about message delivery. Let me put the question to you this way: *How much time a week do you work on your sermon's delivery as opposed to your sermon's assembly?* For most pastors, very little of their preparation is dedicated to delivery.

The sermon is an oral medium. How ironic that a practice so dependent on delivery would have the majority of its practitioners dedicate such small amounts of time (if any) to the week's preparation for it! It's like an opera singer who refuses to develop her vocal execution, an orchestral pianist who never practices scales, or a professional baseball pitcher who decides bullpen sessions aren't for him. Those examples sound ridiculous because they defy reality: each of these professions demands time spent on bettering the execution of that profession. Yet many preachers go throughout their entire message preparation process with little to no intentional focus on the actual delivery of those messages.

Too many preachers take for granted that their Sunday morning delivery needs little improvement. They may think to themselves, "Hey, I got the role of preacher in the first place. Surely that means I'm relatively good at delivery." Avoid this false presumption – there are churches all across the nation led by individuals who can't preach. Nevertheless, that kind of rationale leads to simply another week in the study which is heavily focused on sermon assembly while sermon delivery takes a hit.

This is also unfortunate because, when it comes to preaching, it matters *how* you say *what* you say. Pastors who understand the importance of delivery know that *the whom determines the how.* The *whom*, the ones being spoken to, shapes how something ought to be spoken. Preaching that moves people knows this truth and implements it. The tragedy of the pulpit is when pastors make great content virtually undeliverable to their listeners because they don't consider how congregants best receive those messages during the preaching event. The *whom* determines the *how*. Always.

In that light, this is not a book concentrated on the *what* of your preaching. It is about *how* you preach the *what*. It's about how you can better deliver the content you've created in the hopes that you wind up hitting more wonder shots than duffs. This book is designed to help you find more fairways and less sand traps, to hit the ball straighter and farther, and to leverage your preaching gifts in a way that hopefully leaves you more encouraged and less anxious after you step away from the pulpit each week.

THE 'WHO' MATTERS TOO

Philips Brooks famously defined preaching as truth communicated through personality.[1] This means that in order to address *how* you preach, one must also address *who* is preaching. Do you know who you are as a preacher? Are you responsibly leveraging your personality in the preaching event? Have you discovered your voice in the pulpit, or – using the golf metaphor - do you find yourself regularly borrowing someone else's clubs and trying to imitate their swing in the pulpit?

A lack of self-awareness is one of the greatest hurdles to preaching that moves people. It's a fast track to frustration and exasperation. Pastors will find themselves emotionally, physically,

---

[1]   https://www.preaching.com/articles/past-masters/phillips-brooks-truth-through-personality/ (accessed Aug. 10, 17)

and mentally drained to a greater extent after preaching when they preach outside of themselves. They are communicating truth but not through their own personality. In other words, they have the *what* but are missing the *who*. This is the kind of preaching that is faithful to the content of preaching but isn't connected to the medium which delivers that content: the preacher himself. Preaching that moves people combines well-crafted messages with well-connected messengers. It marries the *how* with the *who*.

That's why this book will not only address the message but the messenger as well. Readers will learn how to identify their unique preaching personality, developing and leveraging that specific personality's voice each and every Sunday. This is key to preaching that moves people. The *who* matters too.

WHAT THIS BOOK IS AND ISN'T ABOUT

I am keenly aware the title *Preaching that Moves People* can be easily misunderstood. Some might be tempted to consign this book to the unwanted stack of others who promote gimmicks over God, strategies over Spirit, or other pragmatic approaches to preaching that are less than biblical. If that were the case, I would be first to toss this effort onto the pile. Therefore, let me begin by acknowledging from the outset two very important truths which are foundational in preaching.

First, I believe God is utterly sovereign in salvation. Jesus clearly said in John 6:65, "No one can come to me unless it is granted him by the Father." There must first be heavenly warrant for anyone coming to him in salvation. In Ephesians 1:11, the Apostle Paul speaks of God's initiatory action in salvation, describing our coming to faith as "having been predestined according to the purpose of him who works all things according to the counsel of his will." We see this necessity for divine work in real-time when, during Paul's preaching of the gospel in Philippi, a Thyatiran businesswoman named Lydia is converted. What was the reason for her conversion as she listened to Paul's message? Acts

16:14 simply states, "The Lord opened her heart to pay attention to what was said by Paul."

While this passage doesn't negate the need for preaching or the responsibility of the listener, it does highlight the biblical truth that God is the one who moves first. It would be easy to continue citing biblical passages which trumpet the sovereignty of God concerning the reception of the gospel by its hearers, but hopefully it's clear that the free and providential work of the Holy Spirit is essential for fruitful preaching. It is always the case, without exception. Everyone who aims to preach with any real effect in the pulpit will need to depend upon the grace of the Spirit's power from start to finish. If the Spirit doesn't move the people, they will not be truly moved.

Our affirmation of God's sovereignty in the preaching event clearly doesn't remove the necessity of a preacher. Romans 10:14 states,

> How then will they call on him in whom they have not believed? And how are they to believe in him of whom they have never heard? And how are they to hear without someone preaching?

Preaching is not an *either/or* proposition. It is both. God, through his grace, effects the divine work of his Spirit on the hearts of listeners through the human work of preaching. In the preaching equation, the Lord has determined that the preacher is just as essential as the God he proclaims. His role is to speak for God. That's one more reason why, in addition to mastering a sermon's theological content and hermeneutical accuracy, the preacher must be adept at sermon delivery.

The second foundational truth I believe about preaching is that Christ is ultimately the content of preaching. In Luke 24, Jesus encountered a pair of his disciples sorely needing some biblical encouragement (believing the Lord had failed to be resurrected). Yet instead of simply revealing himself to these men, Jesus pulled out his pocket Old Testament and then, "beginning with Moses and all the Prophets, he interpreted to them in all the Scriptures the things concerning himself." (v. 27) Amazing! Jesus walked these individuals through the entirety of the Scripture of his day, pointing out all the different ways it displays him.

At any moment in this conversation, Jesus could have easily relieved their sorrow by simply saying, "Here I am!" Instead, he pointed them to the Scriptures and said, "Here I am!" This is not only important for all who call themselves followers of Jesus, but especially those who feel the calling to preach and teach the Bible to Christ's followers. Jesus Christ is the ultimate end of preaching. Period.

Christ highlighted this same truth in John 5:39 when he explained to the religious experts of his day, "You search the Scriptures because you think that in them you have eternal life; and it is *they that bear witness about me.*" Jesus believed the Scriptures to be ultimately about him. If we want to preach the Bible like Jesus read the Bible, we must believe the same as well.

Thus, the preacher will care to demonstrate how Christ and his redemptive work are the sum and substance of the Scriptures. This doesn't mean pastors are called to stay away from delivering sermons which deal with ethical or behavioral issues. They can and should. However, those messages are to be placed within the framework and perspective of the gospel. In other words, the sermon must answer how the reality of the gospel leads, informs, and tutors believers in those behaviors.

While Paul's writing is filled with specific instruction regarding the behaviors that should be present in the life of a Christian, listen to how the apostle summarized his preaching ministry while at the church at Corinth. Before we hear his answer, can we imagine possible sermon series that Paul might have preached to that Asia Minor congregation based on the contents of 1 Corinthians? Let's use a little creative license.

- *We are One: A Series on Church Unity* (Chs. 1-4)
- *Sex Ed 101: Honoring God in Your Sexuality* (Ch. 5)
- *Law & Order: How We Treat Each Other* (Ch. 6)
- *To Be or Not To Be: Marriage & Singleness* (Ch. 7)

- *Food Fights: Issues of Conscience* (Chs. 8-11)
- *Body Parts: Using Your Spiritual Gifts* (Chs. 12-14)

Without a doubt, those sermon series would have messages chock-full of moral exhortations and practical applications. Yet notice how Paul summarized his preaching ministry amongst the Corinthians in 1 Cor. 2:1-2,

> And I, when I came to you, brothers, did not come proclaiming to you the testimony of God with lofty speech or wisdom. For *I decided to know nothing among you except Jesus Christ and him crucified.*

How can Paul say, from a content perspective, he only preached "Christ and him crucified" when, based on his letters, we are confident he addressed all kinds of topics with an eye toward moral and ethical applications? Like Jesus, Paul preached those messages within the framework of the gospel. They weren't merely sermons about marriage, spiritual gifts, or unity – with Jesus possibly sprinkled in at the end like some kind of sermonic footnote – but how each of those issues are rooted and shaped in the person of Jesus and his work at the Cross.

For example, in his writing concerning lawsuits against believers, Paul doesn't merely tell the Corinthians to stop behaving poorly while giving practical ways to act more appropriately. Instead, he ties their interactions with each other to the work of the gospel saying "you were washed, you were sanctified, you were justified in the name of the Lord Jesus Christ and by the Spirit of our God." (1 Cor. 6:11) Once again, Paul wants his listeners' behavior rooted in the beliefs which spring from the gospel and makes an effort to show his listeners how and why their conduct is attached to "Jesus Christ and him crucified."[2]

This is why, from a content perspective, I believe preaching the

---

[2] I think it interesting that the ethically-heavy chapters of 1-14 are bracketed by 1:2 and 15:1-5 whereby Paul stresses the importance and centrality of the gospel to the Corinthian Christians.

Bible – from Genesis to Revelation – must ultimately have Jesus and the work of the gospel at its center.[3] As Charles Haddon Spurgeon, known in his day as the Prince of Preachers, once proclaimed,

> The motto of all true servants of God must be, "We preach Christ; and him crucified." A sermon without Christ in it is like a loaf of bread without any flour in it. No Christ in your sermon, sir? Then go home, and never preach again until you have something worth preaching.[4]

May it be known from the outset of this writing: the Lord is sovereign to save in the preaching event and the content of preaching must ultimately have Christ at its heart. These are my deep convictions. Hopefully this will keep readers from misinterpreting my contribution to preaching as a kind of pushing-the-right-pragmatic-buttons approach, which finds its legitimacy in the ends and not the means. Nothing could be further from the truth.

And yet, the reason I open this book with a confession of specific beliefs about preaching is because this book's focus is on the more practical elements of sermonizing, rather than its theology or content. This work is neither a treatment on Christ-centered hermeneutics nor gospel-centered homiletics. My aim is not to help you see how you can preach Jesus through the entire text or even feel the conviction for such, although I hope you will. It is essential for the kind of preaching that matters.

If you find yourself lacking in this type of training, let me suggest you put this book down and begin with other works whose burden is to train in those critical competencies. I can't stress this strongly enough. Find other resources whose burden is to cultivate preachers in gospel-centered homiletics. Thankfully, there is a wealth of redemptive-oriented preaching resources currently

---

[3] For a better understanding of Christ-centered preaching, I highly recommend the outstanding *Christ-Centered Preaching* by Bryan Chapell.

[4] 7/9/1876; Sermon #2899
(https://blogs.thegospelcoalition.org/justintaylor/2010/08/04/preach-christ-or-go-home-and-other-classic-spurgeon-quotes-on-christless-preaching/; accessed 9/9/16)

available.[5] Once again, that is not the goal of this book. After learning what to say in the pulpit, I can train you to say it well.

A LACK OF ATTENTION

The burden of this text is to address an area in preaching I don't believe is given enough attention. To be fair, there may be resources of which I am unaware, but throughout the course of my undergraduate, graduate, and postgraduate degrees – all of which included training on preaching – I found little to no real training on working through the actual delivery of the message. Most of the evaluations (from both professor and peer) scrutinized the technical side of preaching:

- *Did you have an introduction, body, and conclusion?*
- *Were there points, sub-points, and illustrations to support them?*
- *Was your application clear and easy to understand?*

Make no mistake: these are good and important areas to cover in preaching sermons. They're just not the only ones. This may be why there are so many pastors who are adept at creating technically structured sermons which would receive an 'A' in the classroom – but get an 'F' in the pulpit.

Many pastors struggle in preaching sermons that move people not because the sermons aren't technically sound, but because they're not emotionally sound. While I will explore this later in the book, an emotionally unsound sermon is one where the letter is correct, but the spirit is off. All the instruments are there - just no music. These kinds of messages might get high marks for their components but receive low scores for how those components are

---

[5] In addition to Chapell's *Christ-Centered Preaching*, consider Graeme Goldsworthy's *Gospel-Centered Hermeneutics*, Sidney Greidanus' *The Modern Preacher and the Ancient Text*, Goldsworthy's *Preaching the Whole Bible as Christian Scripture*, Tony Merida's *The Christ-Centered Expositor*, Trevin Wax's *Gospel-Centered Teaching*, and Ed Clowney's *Preaching Christ in All of Scripture*.

arranged to best impact the hearer. This is to see the preacher as technician, not artist.

Pastors can have a sense of their sermon's points but not a feel for its message, due to an unbalanced emphasis on deliverables as opposed to delivery. It's to see the sermon as mere parts and not its sum. This kind of thinking arguably produces preachers more focused on hitting the right spots in their notes than getting a feeling for how those spots rightly hit their listeners. These sermons then struggle to connect with their respective congregations.

There is no doubt what you find in this book has been previously written and spoken about – but likely not very much. In dialoguing with pastors from all across the country, I hear the same refrain after they engage this material on preaching: "I was never taught this. I never heard anything like this in my years of training." The dearth of this kind of emphasis in training preachers wasn't limited to what I personally saw and experienced in my formal training as a young minister. Frankly, I have yet to see it substantively addressed in the last thirty years in my continuing education as a preacher. Again, the key word is *substantively*. Tim Keller, well-known pastor and author, appears to agree:

> Most of our teaching and most of our books on preaching and exposition are fairly unbalanced...almost all the time [they are] dedicated to how to expound the text; how do you understand the truth. There might be a chapter on application or a chapter on preaching to the heart, but...we actually don't spend that much time talking about how you bring the truth home in a way that actually changes lives. It's one of the reasons an awful lot of our expository preaching isn't very life-changing.[6]

But this lack of emphasis concerning delivery and speaking in an emotional sense isn't a new phenomenon. Listen to how Spurgeon felt about the training of preachers in the nineteenth century. In one

---

[6] http://resources.thegospelcoalition.org/library/preaching-to-the-heart (accessed August 11, 2017)

of his lectures to young ministers, he said this about delivery:

> Our subject is one which I find scarcely ever noticed in any
> books upon homiletics — a very curious fact, for it is a most
> important matter, and worthy of more than one chapter. I
> suppose the homiletical *savants* consider that their entire
> volumes are seasoned with this subject, and that they need
> not give it to us in lumps, because, like sugar in tea, it flavors
> the whole. That overlooked topic is, How TO OBTAIN AND
> RETAIN THE ATTENTION OF OUR HEARERS. Their
> attention must be gained, or nothing can be done with them:
> and it must be retained, or we may go on word-spinning, but
> no good will come of it.[7]

This lack of emphasis is still around, and I'm not entirely sure
why. When it comes to seminary, with the numerous areas in which
one must be trained for vocational ministry and the limited
opportunities professors have with students, I imagine that
homiletics professors have wisely chosen to focus on the more
foundational elements of textual exegesis, Christ-centered
hermeneutics, and expositional preaching. If I only had a handful of
classes explicitly dedicated to preaching, I would focus on the
technical aspects of sermonizing as well.

But why the vacuum of resources that deal with, as Keller puts
it, "preaching to the heart" – where we focus more on sermon
delivery and presentation? Maybe such teaching would be too easily
criticized as succumbing to the temptation of pragmatism, or
appearing too theologically dubious and spiritually lightweight. It's
possible no one wants their ideas to be misconstrued as loitering in
emotionalism or manipulation. Maybe it's because you can't find a
Bible verse for each and every statement you make about it.
Ultimately, it doesn't matter. What matters is preachers of every
shade and stripe may find themselves in great need of growing in an
area of their preaching ministry which received little to no attention

---

[7] Charles Spurgeon, Lectures to My Students, Lecture Nine (AGES Software Albany,
OR, Version 1.0, 1996), 141. (Emphasis original)

during their formative years in ministry. They have to develop their delivery. Doing so makes all the difference.

THE ABC'S (AND F) OF PREACHING

My hope is that you will use this book to develop your delivery so you are more apt, by God's grace, to preach in a way that moves people. In the first part, you will be given the tools to feel through your messages as opposed to merely thinking about them. You'll learn how to look for traction, know when too much is too much, and develop a better sense of how your sermon is connecting with listeners. You'll be taught phrases like "get down the mountain" and "emotional flow" to assist you in thinking differently about sermon preparation. These phrases and the concepts that go with them can be arranged into three key sections that form a baseline to helping you preach in a way that moves people. It's as simple as ABC.

✈

ARRANGE FOR TENSION
BUILD FOR SPEED
CHART FOR BANDWIDTH

The second, shorter part of the book will address the kind of messenger who preaches in a way that moves people. This section and its respective chapters come under the big idea of **FINDING YOUR VOICE**. The focus is developing the *who* to match the *what* – the messenger and the messages.

This book isn't written for the uber-gifted preacher. If that's you, you don't need my help. You do what you do in the pulpit intuitively. No, this book is for the other 95%. It is for those who have gifts in preaching at churches both great and small. The ones who know how to exposit the text, support with illustrations, and put it all together in an intelligible, clear sermon - yet still feel there's something amiss. Messages don't flow like they need to, or they are emotionally scattered, or listeners aren't taken on a journey as much as given a presentation.

This book is for those who find themselves faced with the

frustrating inconsistency of having one week where they love the sermon and the next week makes them want to hang it up for good, where what's needed isn't necessarily to work harder at writing sermons but having a different way to look at them. We need to craft sermons that are arranged for tension, built for speed, and charted for bandwidth. We need to preach messages with our own voice, working within our natural emotional boundaries and carrying the listeners "down the mountain" in such a fashion that they can't wait to do it again next Sunday. In short, we need to preach in a way that moves people!

I'm convinced many pastors really don't have much adjusting to do in order to preach those kinds of sermons. They merely need to work through this book, commit to thinking a little differently about preaching, and implement maybe the one or two changes which would make all the difference in the pulpit. You can preach in a way that better moves people. Let me show you how.

ARRANGE
FOR
TENSION

1

PEOPLE-CENTERED
PREACHING

Preaching has two basic objects in view: the Word and the human listener. <u>It is not enough to just harvest the wheat; it must be prepared in some edible form or it can't nourish and delight.</u> [8]
— TIMOTHY KELLER

Over my years in ministry I have heard scores of definitions for preaching and teaching. Some argue that the New Testament knows no difference between the two terms, while others take great pains to articulate a difference. My intention is not to argue for one or the other of these conclusions. However, for the sake of clarity in this chapter, I want to offer working definitions for teaching and preaching:

Teaching is giving information that explains.
*Preaching is calling people to respond
to information that explains.*

---

[8] Timothy Keller, *Preaching: Communicating Faith in an Age of Skepticism* (Viking, 2015), 14.

For example, on Tuesday afternoon a seminary professor lectures his eager students on the doctrine of the atonement. He defines it, shares how various groups understand its scope, and concludes by discussing the impact the death of Christ has on the Christian faith. The period ends. Students rise from their desks and leave for their next class in order to learn other important information.

On Sunday morning, a pastor calls upon his unbelieving congregants to place their faith in the One who atones for sin. He also encourages his believing hearers to deepen their trust in the truth that their sins are forever forgiven because of Christ's work of the Cross, even adding several practical ways his congregants can live out the implications of the atonement. The service ends with all congregants challenged to apply what they have heard expounded from the Scriptures.

There is a difference between these two communicators. The aim of the professor is to give information that explains. The aim of the preacher is to call others to respond to information that explains. It is this call for a response that differentiates the professor from the preacher, and the classroom from the sanctuary. There might be professors who disagree with my assessment, protesting that they too call for a response: to understand and learn what is being taught. But the response pastors seek from their hearers moves beyond intellectual assent. It is something deeper, more comprehensive. J. I. Packer said it this way: "For whereas one lectures to clear heads and ripen minds, one preaches to change lives and save souls."[9]

This is the practical difference between teaching and preaching. All good preaching includes teaching – there are truths within the sermon that listeners must know and understand. However, unless the preacher calls for a response (belief, emotion, action, etc.) to those truths, what happens in the pulpit remains more lecture than sermon. He has not engaged in the act of preaching. Indeed, I contend that messages are given weekly in churches around the

---

[9] J.I. Packer, *Truth and Power* (Intervarsity, 1999), 132.

nation which are really lectures in disguise – there is no real, substantive call to the congregants to respond to what they've heard.[10]

THE WHOM DETERMINES THE HOW

Please don't misunderstand – as I've noted, teaching is an essential part of preaching; it's just not the same as preaching. You can share as many truths as you like on Sunday, but if you are not calling your listeners to do something in light of those truths, then you are not preaching. <u>Good preaching both explains information and calls people to respond to that information.</u>

Additionally, knowing that preaching necessitates calling for a response brings a necessary weightiness to the manner in which we present that information. Far too often, preachers organize their material like lectures rather than sermons, by focusing on the best way to dispense information instead of the best way for people to *respond* to the information dispensed. A difference in purpose should, however, lead to a difference in method.

<u>When it comes to delivery, teaching is *content-centered*.</u> This means the most important objective is to present information in a clear, connected, and comprehensive fashion. That's why in many seminary classrooms, lectures follow an intricately constructed outline beginning with a thesis statement and containing a myriad of points, sub-points, and sub-sub-points. If the objective is to download new information, it makes great sense for the information to be assembled (and presented) with logic and coherency as the highest values. The presentation doesn't have to be emotional, memorable, or captivating because the point of teaching is delivering content for people to *comprehend*, not respond.

But if the objective of preaching is for hearers to act upon the information presented, it necessitates a change in how the content is assembled and delivered. Logic and coherency, critical components as they are, will no longer be the only values considered

---

[10] This isn't an argument for the altar call, but preaching in such a way that demands a response from the listener in some form or another to the message.

– rather the preacher must seek values such as *memorability,*
emotional connection, simplicity, and *captivation.* I contend these
latter components are as essential as logic and order, because the
pulpit is for preaching – not merely teaching. Preachers call people
to respond to what they hear, not simply to absorb it. One can see
that aim in the words of Jonathan Edwards' farewell sermon: "I
have not only endeavored to awaken you...but I have used my
utmost endeavor to win you."[11] Teaching is giving information that
explains. Preaching is an attempt to *win* people to respond to
information that explains.

Therefore, in contrast to teaching, the delivery in preaching is
robustly *people-centered.* Make sure to understand what I am
saying here: it is the delivery, not the content of preaching, which is
people-centered. This is a major distinction. As discussed in the
introduction, the content of preaching has, is, and always should be
centered on Jesus Christ and the work of the gospel. Yet while the
content of preaching is Christ-centered, its delivery is
unapologetically people-centered. Here's the principle of delivery:
the whom determines the how. The *whom* you speak to (audience)
determines the *how* it is spoken (delivery).

Jesus exemplified this truth. Take his healthy use of parables in
his preaching ministry. One dictionary defines the parable as a
"short story that teaches a moral or spiritual lesson."[12] Another
source says parables are stories where "most of the hearers had an
immediate identification with the points of reference that cause
them to catch the point."[13] Simply put, a parable is an effective
communication device because it presents truth wrapped in a
simple story with which hearers could easily identify.

While one could easily make the case that Jesus used parables
both to reveal truth to some and hide it from others (cf., Mt. 13:10),
it's not incorrect to say his use of the parable genre demonstrates

---

[11] http://www.christianity.com/11563506/ (accessed June 23, 2017)

[12] http://www.merriam-webster.com/dictionary/parable (accessed Feb. 26, 2016)

[13] Fee, Gordon and Douglas Stuart, *How to Read the Bible for All Its Worth* (Zondervan, 1993), 139.

that his listeners (i.e., the *whom*) were foremost in his mind when it came to how Christ communicated truth. The Lord's parables leveraged the everyday experiences of his hearers by involving scenes and objects they would be incredibly familiar with. Jesus employed agricultural (e.g., wheat and tares), pastoral (e.g., lost sheep), and other general snapshots of daily life. He also used common images (e.g., mustard seed, fig tree, the Jerusalem mount) that his "congregants" would be able to connect to their own experiences. In sum, Jesus used his listeners' world and their experiences within that world to shape his preaching ministry because he knew what all good preachers know: *Delivery is people-centered.*

His apostles knew this truth as well. Take Paul's speaking ministry in Athens, Greece. Acts 17 finds the apostle preaching at the Areopagus, also known as Mars Hill, which was the meeting place for a court of men who ruled over religious and civil issues in Athens.[14] It also was the spot for Athenians who desired to discuss their ideas about religion, philosophy, culture, and law. In examining the content of Paul's message at Mars Hill, at least two indicators point to the apostle's commitment to people-centered delivery.

First, Paul used his listeners' immediate surroundings. He mentions a nearby altar in v. 23, "For as I passed along and observed the objects of your worship, I found also an altar with this inscription, 'To the unknown god.'" Paul then proceeded to use this well-known, local reference point as a springboard for preaching, because it was a mental image he knew every one of his audience members could engage. For the people-centered preacher, the altar to the unknown god was low-hanging fruit, ripe for the picking to use in his message.

Secondly, Paul, knowing that his *whom* was educated both

---

[14] Some might object to characterizing Paul's speech in Acts 17 as preaching (i.e., the kind we find in local churches on a Sunday), but I am using the operational definition of preaching as a message which calls people to respond to the information presented.

culturally and philosophically, intentionally selected a *how* that doesn't begin with citations from the Old Testament. He instead introduces the works of popular pagan Greek writers. The apostle quotes both the Cretan philosopher/seer Epimenides and the Stoic poet Aratus in vv. 27-28:

> Yet [God] is actually not far from each one of us, for 'In him we live and move and have our being'; as even some of your own poets have said, 'For we are indeed his offspring.'

The rest of the message reveals that Paul intentionally took his listeners through this secular train of thought in order to ultimately lead them to the more explicitly biblical truths of repentance and judgment.

Why does Paul choose this preaching strategy? Why not begin with the Holy Scriptures? This master preacher and evangelist knew that his non-Jewish, highly educated listeners would not only be more familiar with but also more greatly esteem the cultural and philosophical voices of their day than the Jewish Scriptures. Did the apostle's approach belie his confidence in the power and efficacy of the Bible? Hardly. This scene merely demonstrates that Paul's messages were tailored to the people he was trying to persuade for the sake of the gospel. Once again, Paul, like his Lord before him, knew what all great preachers know: a sermon's delivery must be people-centered.

These examples are clear: in the preaching ministries of both Jesus and Paul, when it came to delivery, *the whom determined the how*. The message's recipients are the primary drivers for determining the manner in which the message is preached. Therefore, those who desire to preach in a way that moves people must unapologetically hold to the conviction that while the content of a sermon must always be gospel-centered, its delivery must always be people-centered.

DIFFERENCE BETWEEN MOVING & MANIPULATING

This distinction between content and delivery is important because it is possible to preach with a goal of not moving others but, frankly, manipulating them. Preaching that moves people has people-centered delivery with gospel-centered content, but preaching that manipulates people has people-centered delivery with people-centered content. Manipulative preaching anchors itself to the audience's emotions instead of the truth of Jesus and his gospel. The aim of this kind of dangerous preaching is not to communicate truth which needs a response but to only garner an emotional reaction irrespective of the truth.

Preaching these types of sermons may appear greatly effective with congregants but will have short-lived, ephemeral results. People may be excited in the moment about what they've heard, but – because it isn't tied to the wondrous grace of Jesus' person and work – the sermon amounts to little more than a pep rally whose leader is imploring others to stay committed to their New Year's resolutions. Those types of emotionally-conjured decisions often evaporate by the time everyone cleans up after Sunday lunch.

Dr. Martyn Lloyd-Jones wrote, "There is nothing more hateful than a man who deliberately tries to play on the surface and superficial emotions of people. I have no interest in that except to denounce it."[15] Manipulative preaching messes with the *what* one preaches. It's to trust in the parlor tricks of emotion or Scripture-twisting instead of the Spirit of God to work through the rightly divided Word. It's always a bad idea. John Stott counselled that preachers "are to be neither inventors of new doctrines nor editors who delete old doctrines. Rather, they are to be stewards, faithfully handing out scriptural truths to God's household. Nothing more, nothing less, and nothing else."[16] Stott merely echoes the truth Paul notes in 1 Cor. 2:2, that the ultimate content of Christian proclamation is "Christ and him crucified." The content of gospel

---

[15] Martyn Lloyd-Jones, *Preaching and Preachers* (Zondervan, 2012), 107.
[16] John Stott, *The Challenge of Preaching* (Eerdmans, 2015), 96.

heralds is decided and done. When it comes to preaching, don't mess with the *what*!

However, while the Christ-centered content of a message is untouchable, its delivery can and should be shaped based on the hearers. To have a blind eye toward the relationship between delivery and audience, as we've seen, is to preach in a manner that would have been foreign to Jesus and his apostles. They knew the *what* they needed to preach and determined *how* best to preach that content based on *who* was listening. Pastors who fear manipulating their listeners need only to focus on ways to make sure their *how* best fits their congregants while knowing the *what* never needs changing. Let's look at some ways a preacher's delivery can work in opposition to the goal of moving the hearts of their listeners.

THE EXPLANATION-DRIVEN ARRANGEMENT

Far too many preachers operate as engineers who feel the need to explain everything at the beginning of their messages. They begin their sermons stating their main assertions then over the course of the message proceed to give points and sub-points as to why those assertions are correct. This is a sermon with an explanation-driven arrangement.

As the term indicates, the composition of this kind of message is controlled by its main objective: the explanation of content. Simply put, the sermon's primary intent is to help people understand but not necessarily respond to what is being preached. Therefore, like the professor's lecture, the arrangement of the sermon is often deductive, linear, and easy to follow intellectually.

While these explanation-driven messages may be clear and cogent, their arrangement may also make them less appealing to listeners. What many pastors consider the strength of their messages – the assembly of the content – may actually be a weakness. This only serves to stress the importance behind how one orders the content of sermons.

Unfortunately, for many preachers (especially those with

seminary training) moving in a different direction concerning sermon construction proves a hard task. Their message development mechanics were constructed in classes, tutored by professors, and shaped by books which stressed organizing the message in an orderly fashion. Clarity and coherence were values that ruled the day, where sermons should begin with the main idea, followed by a logical sequence of points (and maybe sub-points) supported by illustrations and applications.

Many have etched in their hearts and minds the homiletical maxim given to countless novice preachers: "Tell them what you are going to tell them, tell them, then tell them what you told them."[17] Others might humorously chime in, saying they were taught a good message is "three points and a poem." Regardless of how the foundation was laid, this concept that the ideal sermon is one where clarity of explanation is the chief guide for construction has a gravitational pull that is almost inescapable. I would humbly suggest, however, that it's a less effective way to organize a sermon.

I once attended a conference where a well-known pastor gave a message on the scope of the atonement. He began by telling everyone what he believed the Bible said about the extent of Christ's work at the cross, then he informed us that the remainder of his message would be the delineation and explanation of the forty points which supported his claim. He even joked somewhat about the sermon's abundant number of points. I nestled into my seat, curious to see how things would play out.

As noteworthy as this individual was, it was only a matter of time before one could see the audience (most of whom held this dear brother in the highest of regards, if not idolizing him) begin to check out from his message. Indeed, as the sermon crept up to points twelve through fifteen, groups of people would excuse themselves from the sanctuary never to return. The empty chairs only increased

---

[17] I've heard this statement ascribed to Aristotle, Dale Carnegie, and others. I'm not sure of its origin, but it definitely has made its way into more than a few seminary classrooms.

as he worked his way toward his fortieth point. By the time he finished, the gaps in the room were embarrassingly noticeable. The experience reminded me that no matter who you are or how great your personal appeal, we can arrange our sermons in such a way that it actually demotivates our congregants from listening. It's not enough to order them for intelligibility or clarity. Explanation isn't the ultimate aim, so sermon organization that only revolves around that value shortchanges what the message could be. We can preach wonderfully clear and insightful sermons that don't move people – and in some cases, it actually *removes* them.

Let me give an example of another message I heard from a very accomplished and effective preacher. The below figure outlines his sermon about the biblical need to plant churches and the qualifications of those who should plant them. I won't include the Scriptural texts used in the message (e.g., 1 Timothy 3:2-7) for ease of better identifying the message's flow or arrangement. The goal here is to understand the sermon's movements. This was the original order of the message:

EXPLANATION-DRIVEN ARRANGEMENT

TENSION: "I WANT TO TELL FOUR STORIES OF CHURCH PLANTERS WHO FAILED."
TENSION RELIEVED: "THE THREE REASONS THESE MEN FAILED ARE...1), 2), 3)."
STORY #1
STORY #2
STORY #3
STORY #4

The construction is straightforward. The preacher begins by asserting both what he is going to address in the message ("I want to tell four stories of church planters that failed.") and his points within the message ("The three reasons these men failed are 1, 2, and 3.").

In this sermon's construction, the answers are given at the beginning. The rest of the message either explains or illustrates the answers. In many circles, this type of sermon arrangement would receive high marks. It has at least followed the first part of the injunction: "Tell them what you're going to tell them." This kind of message order is also easy to follow. If explaining information is the aim of the message, then I would argue this sermon's arrangement is a home run.

The problem, once again, is that explanation should not be the primary aim of the sermon's construction. If preaching is calling people to respond to information we've explained, then the aim should be an arrangement which causes listeners to lean in and take account of what's being said. In other words, the aim of message construction should be *engagement*, not explanation. Unfortunately, the explanation-driven message, almost by design, prevents preachers from capitalizing on engaging their listeners. The strength of the explanation-driven arrangement is also its weakness: a lack of tension. This brings us to the A of the ABC's of preaching that moves people: *Arrange for Tension.*

2

ARRANGE FOR TENSION

You're all clear, kid;
now let's blow this thing and go home!
– HAN SOLO

onsider stories. What makes them so captivating? Why do
people spend time and money watching television shows,
viewing movies, and reading books? Why are some stories
so powerful that they can make you lose all sense of time – you
skipped a shower, forgot to pick up the kids from school, or missed
dinner – because you couldn't bring yourself to put the book down
or stop in the middle of the movie? The stories that stick with us
inherently leverage the power of *tension,* keeping listeners, readers,
and viewers engaged to the end.

Good stories (and storytellers) don't give away all the answers
at the start. They instead allow the audience to engage with a
struggle before the tension is finally relieved. Imagine walking into
the theater to see the original *Star Wars*[18] and, after the opening
credits roll, the audience is immediately transported to Luke
Skywalker flying his X-wing fighter down the famous trench run of
the Death Star. You haven't even eaten your second handful of
popcorn when you witness our young hero fire his proton torpedoes

---

[18] By the original I mean *Star Wars: A New Hope* (1977), of course.

down the enemy installation's exhaust port, resulting in an amazing explosion as the Death Star meets its demise. Do you think that would affect how you watched the rest of the movie?

Or say you decided to binge-watch Peter Jackson's unabridged, director's cut film adaptation of J.R.R. Tolkien's *Lord of The Rings* trilogy. You're geared up on your couch with a month's supply of snacks, ready to be immersed in the epic fight between good and evil in a world called Middle Earth. The opening scene finds the beloved hobbit, Frodo, in his house holding the one ring of power. The musical score intensifies. Jackson's lighting changes and new camera angles reveal that this is an important, even foreboding part of the story. Then, Frodo exits his home to find a Giant Eagle waiting at his doorstep. Our diminutive protagonist proceeds to climb upon the beast who flies him with ease over Mt. Doom whereupon Frodo casually flips the ring into the mountain's destructive fires. *Mission accomplished.* Kind of a buzzkill, don't you think? Now what are you going to do for the next eleven hours or so?[19]

Both examples serve as illustrations of the importance of tension. It's one of the main factors which keeps participants engaged. Tension is like glue: it keeps us stuck to the story. Leveraging it well can be the difference between people leaning in their seats or leaving them. If *Star Wars* or *Lord of the Rings* lose their tension, they demotivate their audiences. That is the reason why the tension – the destruction of evil in both stories – is tethered as closely as possible to the conclusion of the story. The strategy is to keep the audience "glued in" as long it can. It also demonstrates why a story's arrangement has everything to do with leveraging tension well.

Doing so is not some kind of magic or dark art. On the contrary, it's how God has wired us as human beings. Tension arrests us. That's why we dig in for hours at a time with a movie or even spend weeks or months with a book. We want to journey through

---

[19] For the record, one does not simply watch eleven hours of *LOTR* if the ring is destroyed at the start.

something to find the resolution at the end. Take the Bible. Scripture is arranged so that the tension is set from the beginning in Genesis with the fall of man and maintained all the way through the gospel accounts of the New Testament into the book of Revelation itself.[20] Even for God's Word, tension and arrangement go hand-in-hand.

Think of it this way: <u>*Tension*</u> = <u>*Attention*</u>. Keeping one keeps the other. Good stories are arranged to maintain tension as long as possible, and I propose that sermons should seek to do the same. When convinced a sermon's content is Christ-centered and biblically faithful, a preacher should then arrange that sermon with tension, not explanation, as the driving factor. While this may mean setting aside how one was taught sermon construction, I believe it produces a more engaging sermon by a pastor whose goal is to call people to respond to the truth they've heard. It is a big first step to creating a sermon that moves people in the right way for the right reasons.

Let's return to the perfectly logical, coherent message about the qualifications of a church planter we saw in the previous chapter, and examine it with tension in mind. Specifically, let's turn our attention to the beginning of the message.

EXPLANATION-DRIVEN ARRANGEMENT

> <u>TENSION</u>: "I WANT TO TELL FOUR STORIES
> OF CHURCH PLANTERS WHO FAILED."

Notice that the tension of the message is introduced at the start of the sermon. Listeners are told these church planters didn't make it; each of them failed in planting a viable congregation. The tension rises in the room. *Why? What happened? How did it go awry?* No answers are given – only problems.

---

[20] The Cross serves as the turning point, and Christ's Second Coming/New Heavens and New Earth will completely relieve the tension.

Most formal training I've experienced would affirm constructing an introduction in this fashion. I agree as well. Preachers are wise to begin sermons by creating tension for their listeners. Sermon introductions at some level should address: *Why do the hearers need to listen to this message? What is the problem the gospel seeks to solve? Why is this sermon important for the congregants to hear?* All of this should be done. But here is the key: these questions should be posed but *not* answered in the introduction.

Too many sermons do exactly the opposite. Pastors feel the unnecessary need to relieve their message's tension within the first few movements of the sermon. Though this arrangement may appear more effective in explaining the content of what you want to communicate to your congregants, you have seriously impaired their engagement with this content. You essentially blew up the Death Star at the beginning. You destroyed the one ring to rule them all before even taking a step in the journey. In short, you gave all the tension away at the top. Now the listener is less motivated to hear what you have to say. Instead of taking your people on an engaging journey that ends with the answers, they're stuck for the bulk of the sermon listening to your logical, coherent justifications for the answers you already gave them.

The sample sermon does exactly that. It introduces tension then proceeds to immediately relieve that tension.

EXPLANATION-DRIVEN ARRANGEMENT

> **TENSION**: "I WANT TO TELL FOUR STORIES OF CHURCH PLANTERS WHO FAILED."
>
> **TENSION RELIEVED**: "THE THREE REASONS THESE MEN FAILED ARE...1), 2), 3)."

This is where prioritizing explanation kills preaching. Sermons are handicapped when the dominant idea behind the content's organization is the explanation of information. That is the guidance needed for commentaries, lectures, or how-to manuals. Those kinds of mediums have outlines appropriate for their ends: the transmission of information in a logical, systematic fashion. Generally speaking, tension isn't factored into how their materials are arranged because, again, explanation – not engagement – is primary. In the land where explanation is king, tension might even be an enemy. It's not seen as a tool to be leveraged, but rather a thorn to be removed immediately. However, a sermon should be the citizen of a different realm, serving another ruler.

Unfortunately, many preachers don't see it that way. They tend to build sermons like professors build lectures and engineers create instruction manuals – little on tension, high on explanation. It may be possible that you have people in your pews with systematic, detail-oriented mindsets who are attracted to the technical reasons behind the answers you gave away at the beginning of your message. They might lean in and stay with you for the entire message, but it's likely your sermon arrangement demotivated the majority of your congregants – who have a God-given wiring for story – from listening intently to the rest of the message.

Explanation-driven arrangements may be why your listeners characterize your sermons as something less like messages and more like lectures. These are usually the times when you leave the pulpit dumbfounded, because you were confident that your content was solid. The sermon was clear and organized; it even had an insightful illustration or two – so what happened? Content alone won't win the day. It's important. It's essential. But if you don't arrange that content to maximize for engagement, your people won't feel it like you feel it when you step into the pulpit each week. The tragedy of that Sunday is your arrangement didn't do your content justice.

THE TENSION-DRIVEN ARRANGEMENT

If preaching is calling people to respond to the information we've explained, then arranging our sermon material with their engagement in mind should be the priority. To organize the components of our message for maximum engagement, we need to think *story*. Let's re-examine our sample message but now with a tension-driven arrangement.

TENSION-DRIVEN ARRANGEMENT

TENSION: "I WANT TO TELL FOUR STORIES OF CHURCH PLANTERS WHO FAILED."
STORY #1
STORY #2
STORY #3
STORY #4
TENSION RELIEVED: "THE THREE REASONS THESE MEN FAILED ARE...1), 2), 3)."

The sermon begins with tension by introducing the statement about four church planters who failed, but the reasons for these failures aren't given up front. The failures themselves are then illustrated in the subsequent stories. The explanation of why these men failed as church planters isn't given until the end, after all the stories are told. For the majority of the message, there is no relief. No time is spent defending the pastor's conclusions, because conclusions haven't yet been reached.

The bulk of the sermon body only deepens the listeners' need to know why these men failed and what can be done about it. They are more likely to pay greater attention and lean in both intellectually and emotionally because they are wired by God with a need for resolution. They are still waiting for the Death Star to explode, anxiously anticipating the time when the one ring melts away. Tension equals attention!

This can be the difference between a sermon that keeps people on the edge of their seat and one that lulls them into wondering what's for lunch. The only difference is an intentional arrangement of the sermon's content to leverage tension, rather than alleviate it. Notice the simple change:

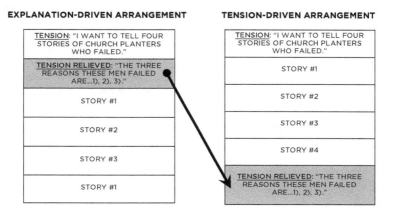

This example moved just one element and completely changed the dynamic of the message. Sometimes simply rearranging the order of your sermon can result in an emotionally engaging message, without doing any significant additional work. Many sermons could be transformed from okay to exceptional if just one element was shifted to a position that maintained tension, rather than relieving it. It isn't necessarily hard, it just requires intentionality. You have to purposely look at your sermon in a different way and ask yourself the question: How do these sermon components create tension and keep that tension throughout the message?

This applies to every element of your message, with no component excused from consideration. For example, would a specific illustration have more emotional impact by moving it somewhere else? Does it create questions or answer them? This examination will help determine where best to place it in the message. I've seen sermons increase their dynamism dramatically simply by moving an illustration for the purpose of better engagement. When organizing your message, it's open season on every component. Move elements to move people.

Challenge yourself to take one message and give it three different arrangements. Don't add any new content; simply reorder the content you already have. Spend time preaching those varied arrangements and see if you can't feel the difference between them. That's the power of arrangement – and why preaching that moves people arranges for tension.

Tension-driven arrangements give the message's concluding resolution greater weight in *the mind of your listeners*, because you spent more time building the desire for that answer in *the hearts of your listeners*. It gives teeth to your conclusions and traction to your insights, allowing resolutions to be more deeply embedded in your audience. These benefits are far superior to those offered by an explanation-driven sermon.

I continually remind the preaching team at my church to not relieve the tension in their introductions. On the contrary, I want them to create tension initially, then push it down as far as they can in their messages. This means not only holding back on the answer at the introduction of the message, but waiting as long as possible throughout it. Remember, tension equals attention. Keeping the former better ensures keeping the latter.

When I was a child, my parents gave me a unique game. It was a board dotted with holes upon which you inserted different electronic pieces. You began at the left side of the board, inserting and attaching bits that eventually would connect to a small light bulb at the opposite side. If the connections worked, the light would come on. But it wasn't enough just to illuminate the lamp: the better the arrangement, the greater the power – and the brighter the light would shine. I would constantly rearrange the different elements on the board in order to get the best configuration for the brightest light possible. Simply having an order wasn't the aim; I wanted to find the *best* order.

Arranging for tension is a similar quest. It's the preacher's effort to find the best order for his content by merely moving elements to increase the sum of their power. The better your arrangement pushes the tensions down the sermon, the more attractional power the message will have. Don't give sermons with five-star content two-star arrangements. The light might shine, but it could be so much brighter! Arranging for tension can be the difference between a message that simply informs and preaching that moves people.

BUILD
FOR
SPEED

3
BUILD FOR SPEED

I preached as never sure to preach again,
and as a dying man to dying men.
— RICHARD BAXTER

Ever have a moment like this in the pulpit? You are preaching your heart out. Everything is going swimmingly. You feel emotionally connected to your message, and the congregants are leaning in to everything you say. The entire experience feels incredibly encouraging.

Then, out of nowhere, everything changes. Suddenly you sense the sermon beginning to drag. It feels like you are preaching in quicksand. There is no traction to your message as thoughts grow thick, and the delivery of those thoughts even thicker. The message sputters and chokes as you try in desperation to regain the momentum you had mere moments ago. With each passing second, the disconnection from your hearers grows exponentially – eyes begin to wander, heads tilt in any direction but yours, and a blossoming restlessness fills the rows. The shift in the sanctuary is so tangible you could almost touch it. That tinge of unease swings to disappointment. You realize the message is a lost cause. It's so disheartening that stepping down from the pulpit actually brings relief. All you are left with is the nagging question: *What just happened?*

Sure, some parishioners will comment afterward how wonderful your message was; these are the same sweet saints who give you encouragement after every Sunday's sermon. You could preach an hour-long esoteric, mind-numbing, academic message whose stupefying powers of boredom would reduce the lifespan of your congregation by a decade, and those same natural-born encouragers would still place their hand on your shoulder, smile at you, and remark, "Wonderful job today, pastor!" But you know better. The sentiments are appreciated, but there's no doubt that the message fell flat.

Monday brings you back to the drawing board, but this time you begin your message preparation with great trepidation, trying to figure out what went wrong and how to avoid it. There can be many different reasons for this kind of frustrating experience in the pulpit. I don't pretend to offer a panacea for every sermon which perishes in the quicksand of delivery. However, I do believe there is a primary reason why many preachers find themselves in this kind of predicament. It doesn't entail growing in your hermeneutical skills or finding better illustrations. More often than not, avoiding quicksand in the pulpit has to do with speed, pace, and a sense for how things flow in the sermon.

This brings us to the second letter of the ABC's of preaching that moves people: *Build for Speed.* If you want to preach a message which not only connects with your congregants but also maintains that connection, you will need to learn how to construct the sermon with a keen eye for pace.

Every sermon has a speed to it, a pace that carries the listener along with it. Good messages move people at a rate which helps them embrace the emotion of the message while keeping them connected to its content. In equipping preachers toward this endeavor, I employ a mental model to help them both understand and apply the practice of working with pace in their messages: *getting down the mountain.*

THE MOUNTAIN

One of my favorite things to do is snow ski. From my childhood to present day, there are fewer activities I enjoy more than deftly cascading down a mountain, hearing the swish of the freshly fallen snow parting between my skis. It's a bonus that my lovely wife feels the same way. Some of my favorite moments in my life have been skiing with my bride. A close second is when we ski with friends, especially when everyone possesses generally the same skill-level. We can choose runs with various degrees of difficulty without hesitation and ski at whatever pace we desire, knowing we won't lose anyone in the process.

My wife and I also enjoy skiing with those of a more novice skill level. We love to see beginners grow in confidence and enjoyment as their abilities develop. Plus, truth be told, skiing with novices is a little easier on our bodies as we hit middle-age. However, as much as we love to ski in groups, our approach to the slopes changes when we're accompanied by skiers with less experience.

Imagine the thrill of getting to lead a bunch of your friends down a ski trail they have never tackled before. You are excited not only to do the run for yourself but also to have the joy of helping friends maximize their experience. You want to guide them through the best sections of the run – over this hill, through that chute, around that bend, etc., in such a fashion that they don't get bored, stuck, or lost.

Leading well means maximizing the best the mountain has to offer those following behind you. However, this new journey will only work if *everyone* both accomplishes and enjoys it. It's a loss if only two out of your ten friends actually arrive at the bottom with you. It's also a loss if those two, because of how you led them, had such a bad experience that they never want to ski with you again. Taking others down the mountain demands maintaining group integrity while maximizing the group's adventure. Success isn't merely not losing someone, but also having everyone experience the thrill the mountain has to offer. To do this means leaders have to ski down the mountain in a very specific way.

Preaching is a similar endeavor. The task of the preacher is to guide people "down the mountain" of his sermon: bringing them through your introduction, body, and conclusion so that hearers are not only with you at the bottom of the hill but have maximized their journey getting there. Doing this well means listeners are engaged at every part of the "run": the truths of the Scripture, the illumination of the illustrations, the wonder of the gospel. Preaching is not only science but art. We must become guides who deftly lead our listeners through the wonders, glories, and truths of the preached Word. Essentially, preachers are to master the art of leading others down the mountain of their messages.

In order to do that, preachers – like ski guides skilled at leading a group – must first *chart a path* down the run they believe maximizes the group's experience. Good guides don't begin leading others by tipping their skis over the edge hoping to hit a few good spots if they're lucky. They begin by standing at the edge, surveying the hillside for the best places to go – where their followers not only will stay with them but also can relish the best the run has to offer. Thus, excellent guides chart a path down the mountain.

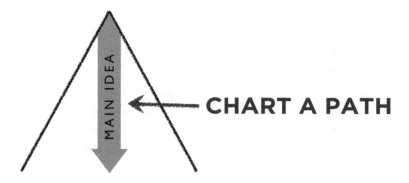

In a sermon, we would call this pathway the main idea.[21] It's the terrain upon which we must guide congregants to experience the

---

[21] a.k.a. One Thing, One Main Thing, Big Idea, One Big Idea, Main Point, etc.

message we intend to preach. This path includes the entirety of our sermon: the introduction, body, and conclusion. It also incorporates every truth, illustration, and story. It's the path to which we must surely stick in order to find the joyous heart of the run while not losing anybody as we journey toward the message's end.

Another reason I use the mountain analogy is that in skiing, you're taught that one of the best ways to manage a run is to *pick a spot at the bottom* and work your way there. This spot becomes the end-goal of the run – where you want your fellow skiers to be when the journey concludes. In preaching terms, the bottom of the mountain is the response you want hearers to have at the message's conclusion. This includes their actions, thoughts, and emotions. In short, what do you want your listeners to do, think, and/or feel after hearing the message? How would you like the congregation to apply what they've heard?

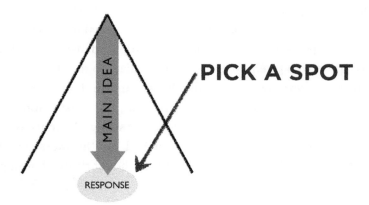

Notice this application isn't bound to one category. A sermon may be a call to some combination of a change in a particular behavior, feeling a certain way, or believing a specific thing. While these may fall into separate categories for the message preparation process, each often bleed into one another.

Remember, picking a spot is important if we want to guide others well. Consider what you desire for the sermon to accomplish.

If preaching is calling others to respond to information, what response are you calling for? The answer you form will be the end point of the journey, the "spot" – the place where you've tried, by God's grace, to bring your congregants via the sermon.

Picking a spot for our hearers doesn't mean we can create those responses or convictions in them. Only the Spirit can do this work. Spiritually genuine, heart-wrought responses to our sermons are solely God's jurisdiction. Nevertheless, preaching is the mystery of joining God in the great endeavor of doing his work and will. It does pastors no good to dismiss strategic thinking about a sermon's objectives as some kind of unspiritual, or even anti-spiritual chore. Thinking through things like picking a spot for your message is how, in the words of the Apostle Paul, we better accomplish the goal to "persuade others" via the preaching of God's Word (2 Cor. 5:11).

Having a clear idea of the response you would like to see in the hearts and lives of your listeners gives a greater intentionality to your sermon preparation. It helps you figure out the best path down the mountain by serving as a filter for decision-making about where on the slope you want to ski. For example, if using a specific illustration won't help to guide your listeners to do, think, or feel what you believe the sermon should accomplish, then you should avoid that section of the run by dropping the illustration from the message. Don't complicate things by using elements which actually work against the goals you had for the message. We guide others well by picking a spot and thoughtfully planning a route to bring them there.

A CONTINUUM OF PACE IN THE MESSAGE

Once the preacher has picked a spot and charted a path toward it, he must actually "ski" through his sermon. He must preach. This brings us to a final aspect of the mountain analogy: *pace*. If you want to preach in a way that moves people, your message needs to possess the right pace. There is a rate of speed or flow that matches the content of every message, and I believe finding that pace is one of the most neglected areas of sermon delivery. I would even argue that one of the main culprits behind sermons that mysteriously crash and burn in the pulpit can be traced to problems with pacing.

This is surely true of skiing with friends. There is a tension when leading a group down the mountain: the pace must be fast enough for people to enjoy the thrill of skiing, but slow enough for lesser skiers to actually keep up without becoming overwhelmed or discouraged. If I go too swiftly over tough terrain, I may look back and see some of them halfway down the hill with only their legs sticking out of the snow. If I move too slowly, I may witness others so deep in the throes of boredom that they quit on me before we get to the bottom, taking off to do something they deem more worthwhile. If they do stay with me, it's only because they don't want to hurt my feelings or there's nowhere else to go. Their fidelity to the journey I'm bringing them on won't be because it was a fulfilling experience for them. It's also likely that they will be less motivated to travel with me in the future. With either group, I lose as a guide if I go too fast or too slow. I must find the right pace for getting down the mountain.

A PACE TOO FAST

This same continuum is found in the pacing of sermons. Your messages can suffer from too quick of a pace.

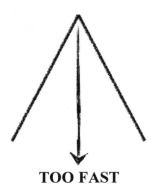

TOO FAST

This type of message is great with the main idea but does a poor job in fleshing it out. It's too "thin" of a sermon because the listener is robbed of the full experience of the truths within the message – truths meant to be deeply plumbed, savored, and treasured. Using the mountain analogy, the sermon has too few turns. The pastor arrives at the bottom prematurely because he didn't leverage the wonder and beauty of the run. It's a wasted opportunity on Sunday. In reflection, this kind of experience for the congregants constitutes the "what might have been" sermon.

It's the type of preaching that can get characterized as a sermonette for a Christianette. More like an extended devotional, it isn't just simple but simplistic. There is no space for any insightful nuance or weighty moment that listeners can dwell upon, because no one is ever there for a long enough period of time. No depths are probed, no ideas fleshed out.

For example, the sermon may have three points, but the time given to those points is so brief that none of them had a chance to be anchored in the listeners' hearts. There may be little to no substantive illustrations, supporting Scriptures, or stories that helped fix the truths of the message in the congregants' minds. On the contrary, the preacher is more concerned about people getting through the points than the points getting through the people. The lack of turns in both number and substance leave little to no place for the Holy Spirit to work through the preaching event. The pace was too fast, and as a result, the sermon and its hearers suffer. Congregants come to the end of this run down the mountain and ask, "Was that it?"

A sermon that's too fast-paced could also be one where the text of Scripture is leveraged poorly. The Bible becomes merely a springboard for the preacher, with little time spent expounding the text itself. The pastor briefly employs God's Word then spends the rest of the message opining about this or that. On the other hand, it's possible that the sermon utilizes multiple passages of Scripture but never truly exposits any of them. In either example, congregants are cheated because they never experience enough quality time with the very thing the Spirit uses to bring change: the Word of God.

These listeners won't know the Bible any better than they did before they sat down, for they haven't been allowed to stay "in the turn" of the Scripture long enough. The pace is too quick. And while everyone may be down the mountain at the end, the preacher doesn't maximize the journey for them. Listeners can't enjoy the richness or fullness of the truth that the message purports to share. The pace of the preaching is too fast.

A PACE TOO SLOW

While there are definitely preachers who struggle with preaching sermons that are too fast, the majority I meet have an altogether different struggle with getting down the mountain of their messages. They wrestle with preaching sermons with a pace that is too slow.

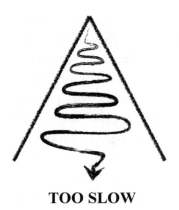

TOO SLOW

This type of sermon is given by preachers who deeply desire that listeners experience the fullness of the truths presented, but the message gets bogged down due to the sheer number of turns. Consequently, the sermon is too "thick." Listeners can't enjoy content because they get lost in it. In the skiing analogy, your followers get stuck somewhere on the mountain because they can't remove themselves from the dense terrain you trudged through or because you've spent too much time on a specific part of the slope when you should have changed direction. This kind of message makes preachers feel really good because they believe they have maximized the slope of the sermon. But when they turn around after arriving at the slope's conclusion, they only see a third of their group has made it down with them. And the sturdy few who did are contemplating if they want to ever take a journey like that again with you.

One reason that your sermon's pace may slow is because you're simply taking too many turns on your run down the mountain. Instead of a few key points, the message has such a large amount of points (remember the 40 points on the atonement?) that there is virtually no way anyone will remember them by the time they finish Sunday lunch. The pastor's only hope is that some of them took notes, but most of us know that those notes will likely get thrown in the trash or filed away, never to see the light of day again.

Your sermon may also be taking too many turns because some of your points are redundant – you've skied that terrain before, and now you're skiing it again. You may not recognize the repetition, but your congregation can feel it. This is another place where you can lose your listener. Some of the message's extra points could have been better reframed as a statement or two under a previous message point. Possibly the sermon didn't need that turn (or turns) at all, because it had little or nothing to do with the main idea. It was off-topic, deviating from the charted path. The turn might have been appealing in the study, but preaching exposes its disconnection from the sermon's main idea. This kind of sermon construction almost guarantees a message whose pace is too slow.

The second and more common problem with slow-paced messages is not the number of turns but the inordinate amount of time spent in them. If the too-fast message doesn't spend enough time in its movements, the too-slow sermon does the opposite. It gives an excessive amount of time to necessary, on-topic turns which, consequently, reduces the effectiveness of those very turns.

For example, a preacher may choose to illustrate a point by telling not one but three stories, all of which accomplish the same goal. Unfortunately, because each illustration accomplished the exact same purpose, the congregants lost interest in the message halfway through the middle story. They got the point the first time, but the guide kept going over the same terrain again and again. Although a preacher may have discovered fifty different passages to support the second point in his outline, sharing them all will overwhelm his listeners and cause them to miss the point he sought to make. Instead of a pertinent passage or two, congregants are taken on a mind-numbing tour of so many books of the Bible that they can't keep track – lessening the impact of the sermon rather than improving it.

In both cases, the turns grew too long and lost people. It's not that the movements in those messages were bad; it's just that the length they possessed reduced the effectiveness of the message. The pace of the preaching is too slow.

It is usually these types of long turns that – at the risk of mixing metaphors – lead us into quicksand moments while preaching. Remember the situation I described at the beginning of this chapter: you're in the pulpit experiencing the joy of working through your hard-wrought sermon. Everyone is engaged. Then suddenly the room seems to go dead – a loss of connection so tangible you can feel it in the pulpit. Preaching now becomes a chore. Instead of looking to the clock with the hope that you have more time to preach, you wish the minutes would tick by faster so that the misery will end.

Preachers often find themselves in this predicament because their messages had either nonessential turns or necessary turns which took too much time. Too many turns or overly long turns will create messages with pacing problems.[22] As the quicksand thickens, your listeners will get bogged down rather than carried along with you

---

[22] If the message has both – too many turns which are also too long – it's probably best to find a support group after the preaching event, because you likely will turn around and see no one with you at the bottom of the mountain. You probably need to call the ski patrol as well.

– and once your pace is lost, it's almost impossible to recover it.

FINDING THE RIGHT PACE

It should be obvious that preachers should aim for a sermon with the right pace. This type of message flows well, moving in and around the main idea with the right amount of turns.

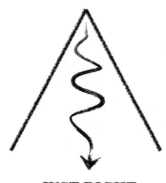

JUST RIGHT

The journey matches both the emotional tenor of the message and the biblical texts presented, its flow carrying listeners through the sermon's points so that they feel the full import of the message. The turns in a well-paced sermon are not only balanced in length but on-topic as well, leading listeners on a well-chosen route toward the response that you are calling them to do, think, or feel.

As a result of well-ordered and keenly built turns, listeners experience the fullness of the message. They not only all reach the bottom of the mountain alongside you, but each of them participates in all the run had to offer. This bodes well for you as a preacher: not only have your listeners had a meaningful experience today, but they will also be more likely to trust you on future journeys through God's Word. For upcoming runs, they may even invite their friends to join you. Doesn't that make your heart beat faster?

THE QUESTION TO ASK

Planning a sermon's pace is essential for preaching in a way that moves people. In your message preparation, ask yourself this important question:

How am I getting down the mountain?

What kind of pace does your message possess? Are you getting down through your sermon too fast or too slow? What do your turns look like? How many do you have and how long do you stay in them?

If you find that your pace is generally too fast down the mountain, you may need to work harder at finding stories, illustrations, supporting Scriptures, etc. to properly extend the turns in the message. Lengthening your turns will help your listeners get the most they can out of your message's main idea. If you continually find yourself moving too slow down the mountain, it may be because you have too many turns, or the turns themselves are too long. It could even be both! You may need to work on removing illustrations, stories, theological digressions, soapboxes, or (dare I say it) overly-burdensome chunks of exposition on specific biblical texts.

As I stated earlier, it is my experience that the majority of pastors who struggle with pace don't preach sermons which are too fast, but too slow. They can't seem to get out of the rut of a message preparation process that leaves them with thick, clunky, and unbalanced sermons. Don't lose hope if this describes the majority of your Sunday efforts! In the next chapter, I give pastors a way forward to thin out their messages in order to gain the pace those sermons need.

4
GAINING PACE

He's going the distance
He's going for speed.
— CAKE, 'GOING THE DISTANCE'

I belong to a church-planting network which has, in my opinion, some of the best preachers on the planet. There doesn't seem to be any formula or pattern to be deciphered here as to why. Some are young; others are older. There are those who lead megachurches with thousands of parishioners, while others shepherd congregations of a couple hundred. Gifted preachers can be found throughout the network's spectrum of different ethnicities and nationalities. Frankly, my tribe has an embarrassment of riches when it comes to the sheer number of powerful, moving, effective preachers within it.

However, this is not the case for every member of our network. Despite the many productive preachers we have in our fold, we also possess beloved pastors who struggle in the pulpit. After listening to a large sampling of sermons from different preachers in my tribe, those who struggle have a dominant characteristic that stands out: the sermons are too slow. This lack of preaching pace tends to produce messages that come across to congregants as thick, sluggish, obtuse, and frankly, really boring.

While other factors may be at play, I believe the chief culprit for meandering, slothful pacing is frequently tied to sermon construction. In using the mountain analogy, one could diagram these kind of messages as follows:

This is the sermon that, soon after its initial effort down the mountain's run, aimlessly traverses in all kinds of directions, if not to a different mountain altogether. The main idea (if there was one) might even splinter into several main ideas along the way.[23]

Maybe the exposition becomes so dominant and expansive that the sermon essentially devolves into some sort of running commentary. This is the kind of sermon where each theological nuance, exegetical tidbit, or doctrinal whim is a butterfly the pastor feels compelled to chase. Another reason for so many turns could be that the stories and illustrations employed in the sermon are legion. Whatever the reason behind the message construction, this misdirected journey usually demands a longer sermon length in order to fit everything. Consequently, at the end of the run, hearers not only find themselves in a different place than they expected, but at the base of a completely different mountain altogether. The end of the message brings confusion, if not exhaustion as well. Needless to say, these types of messages are constructed to fail. It's how to preach in a way that moves people...out the door, likely to never return.

---

[23] If your message has a main idea that becomes main ideas, you don't have *main* ideas anymore. You are only left with ideas.

Gazing at the diagram tempts me to laugh. It would be funny if the messages weren't so dishearteningly unfruitful for both preacher and congregation. Pastors are left wondering why only the most ardent parishioners seem to connect with what was said, while the majority of the congregation is at best unmoved and at worst bewildered. The reason should be painfully clear. These sermons suffer because they lack the critical element of pacing. Well-meaning preachers who consistently preach poorly-paced sermons won't produce a thriving pulpit ministry. Even more tragic, congregations who are given a steady diet of poorly-paced messages might begin to believe this is what it means to preach the Word of God. My friends, this is not supposed to be the fruit of our preaching ministry.

KEEP THEOLOGIANS AS THEOLOGIANS

Some would defend this kind of meandering-on-the-mountain preaching because it mirrors the wonderful thoughts and ideas of the theologians they follow. The desk in the pastor's study is littered with books of favorite authors and thought-leaders. By the end of the week, sermon notes are jam-packed with excursions through this or that deep doctrine, complex idea, or incredibly abstract theological concept. The pastor is excited about Sunday because he is confident that people will be thrilled by the wondrous escapade he has planned. Then Sunday morning comes and goes with a dud, with the pastor questioning what could have possibly gone wrong. I mean, it worked for Calvin and Luther.

There is a difference between preaching a sermon for your local church and delivering a message better suited for a theological convention. To confuse the two will only hamstring the pastor's preaching ministry. Don't misunderstand – I'm not saying to divorce yourself from reading books and listening to preaching that is better suited for a presentation at the Evangelical Theological Society, nor am I advocating the preaching of theologically-lite, fluffy sermons. But if preaching aims to be people-centered in its delivery, you will struggle in the pulpit if your model for constructing sermons more befits a gathering of theological scholars than a local church of laypersons. Your Sunday morning people aren't usually self-professed theology geeks, wearing 'smedium' t-shirts emblazoned with stylistic head shots of their favorite patristic church leader as they scan the internet for the next symposium on some important but rather exclusive doctrinal issue they'd love to debate until 3AM over the perfect cup of fair-trade, single-origin, locally-roasted coffee. It's more likely your congregants are doctors, farmers, retirees, software developers, students, factory workers, engineers, homemakers, businessmen, or other individuals who come to Sunday services simply trying to honor Jesus by hearing and obeying the Word rightfully taught.

This should tutor how we shape our messages for pacing and the kind of preachers we seek to model. Find sermonizers who know how to get down the mountain well. My wager is they will be those whose sermons are primarily targeted to laymen, not armchair theologians. It will serve you well to keep your theological heroes and preaching heroes distinct.[24] Read books by the former, and listen to sermons by the latter. Confusion between the two is one reason why many well-intentioned pastors flounder in their preaching ministries. They take their charge in sermon construction from the professorial stylings and detailed content of a theological lecture where, due to the necessary depth and breadth of content, slow pacing is almost requisite. It takes time to follow abstract theological thoughts, process the mysterious doctrines at hand, and articulate the latest scholarly interactions within it. Great for a lecture hall. Bad for a church sanctuary.

If this is more your style, write a commentary or book. Lead a seminar or class at your local church. Take up blogging. Just don't preach this way to your congregants who, by and large, wouldn't get too excited at hearing Calvin's *Institutes of the Christian Religion* is

---

[24] This doesn't mean they can't be both, but it is a rarer quality than one might think.

being re-released in a Cordovan leather edition.[25] If the only ones who are with you in the pew after hearing you wax poetic on the wonders of sublapsarianism happen to all be wearing the same hip *name-this-dead-church-leader* t-shirts, know you've got more work to do! Trying to preach theology for theologians instead of parishioners will put more turns in your message than a corkscrew, creating a pace that will be too burdensome for the message, or your hearers, to bear. <u>Remember that the goal is to guide people – regular, everyday peop</u>le – down the mountain, so aim to construct a message that maximizes both the experience of the run and the number of people with you at the end of it. This will demand you pick up the pace. The key is to learn how to quicken your pace without coming across as hurried to your listeners.

THE KEYS TO GAINING PACE

Increasing pace begins at the foundational level of message construction. The goal for those who consistently preach messages which feel slow and chunky is to build the message for speed – not to be fast per se, but to be faster so as to properly carry one's hearers down the mountain together and in one accord. I tell preachers to focus on two areas to increase the pace of their sermons.

The <u>first is simplicity</u>. Every preacher needs to come to grips with the idea that "being simple" is his friend. Always fight complexity! As I noted, leave it for books to write or lectures to give. Complexity is the series of troublesome moguls which will only serve to frustrate the listener's ability to follow you down the mountain. It is one of the most common ways to lose people.

Achieve simplicity by removing some turns. This will increase your pace and give the message greater momentum to carry your hearers, both mentally and emotionally. You can also simplify the message by shrinking the length of a turn, using less material within an individual element of your message. For example, instead of having three illustrations to support a point, use only one. You can

---

[25] I'd take one though. I mean, *The Institutes* in Cordovan leather? C'mon!

spend a little more time stretching and filling out one illustration rather than giving space in your message that three illustrations would take. Being simple is about reducing turns or removing turns. It's the easiest way to handle the problematic patches as you lead others down the mountain.

The second area to build sermons with increased pace dovetails with the first: ruthlessness. The gains in speed that simplicity brings can only be achieved if you are ruthless in cutting out stuff you love (those fascinating turns!) from your sermon. Stow the material away for another Sunday. As you might imagine, this demands a sacrifice from the preacher. There is an emotional element to preaching that has nothing to do with the audience but centers on the pastor himself: he is more attached to his sermon than he probably realizes.

Recently, one of our pastors showed me a sermon he had spent the week working on for the upcoming Sunday. It was a well-constructed message with four incredible points. These truths were definitely beneficial for our people and, on top of that, aligned well with the main theme of the message. It was just too much content – my friend would've needed a mountain the size of Everest to say everything he had prepared. When he asked me what I thought he should do, I chose just one of his four points and told him to start skiing.

He hesitated at first. For those who aren't keen on being ruthless, there is almost always some kind of pause. It seems counterintuitive to remove hard-fought material one feels is so important to the message. But people only get what you give them. There is no message until it's preached. Thus, as far as it concerns the congregation, there is no real loss. Only the preacher himself feels the pain of subtraction. My friend's sermon was too thick and slow, desperately needing more pace. The sermon begged for simplicity, and ruthlessly removing content was the only way to achieve it.

He took my counsel and preached the message with only one

point. The result was palpable. Not only did the Lord use the sermon in a powerful way, but my friend could tell a tangible difference in the preaching of it. The message felt more focused, easier to handle, and carried a pace with it that matched the content's emotional flow. The congregants were locked in the entire time – eyes focused, heads leaning forward. My friend left the pulpit this time, not in befuddlement of why things felt thick and dragged along, but with a humble confidence about what transpired in the sanctuary that Sunday. This message moved people because the preacher, as hard as it was emotionally for him, committed himself to ruthless simplicity.

FIGHTING YOUR INNER CONTENT JUNKIE

The story highlights a problem I see with preachers including myself: we are content junkies. We love the stuff that makes up our messages, and we should. However, the temptation is to believe that everything we discover in the study should directly translate to what we preach in the pulpit. Not doing so can feel like a waste, but this perspective is antithetical to creating sermons which effectively get down the mountain.

Stephen King isn't a pastor, and I don't believe anyone would confuse him with one – including King himself. But no one can deny that he is both a prolific writer and a successful storyteller. In his book, *On Writing*, King speaks about the need to jettison anything in one's creation that doesn't move the story along. He counsels authors, "If it works, fine. It if doesn't, toss it. Toss it even if you love it. Sir Arthur Quiller-Couch once said, 'Murder your darlings,' and he was right."[26] Too harsh? Hardly. What is true of writing novels is true of writing sermons.

Preachers too frequently deliver bloated, chunky, or dense messages that are difficult for congregants to process simply because they refuse to cut content from their manuscripts. This is the classic drawback of content junkies. The tragedy is that they are more in love with their content than its reception. As a recovering

---

[26] Stephen King, *On Writing: A Memoir of the Craft* (New York: Scribner, 2000), 197.

content junkie myself, I know the finalized sermon manuscript can feel akin to having a chest full of golden nuggets after dirtying yourself in the depths of the earth for the better part of a week. You are proud of what you find and the effort it took to find it.

Cutting content is painful because it's almost personal, and it's surely costly. Consequently, when faced with removing points, illustrations, or anything else that makes up the message, content junkie pastors doth protest much. King reflects on how his own tribe reacts when called to cut content: "When a novelist is challenged on something he likes – one of his darlings – the first two words out of his mouth are almost always 'Yeah but.'"[27] I hear the same response from preachers when asked to cut content in order to increase the sermon's pace. Honestly, I hear the same thing from myself:

- *Yeah but that's such an important doctrine!*
- *Yeah but that's such a wonderful story to include!*
- *Yeah but I don't think the sermon will work unless I have every one of those seven points!*
- *Yeah but I spent five hours on that specific section!*

I worked hard for that nugget. I came up with that nugget. I love that little piece of gold! Why shouldn't the sermon have every piece of gold I discovered? But great preaching isn't only finding nuggets to bring with you into the pulpit but deciding which of them to leave behind. To my faithful fellow preachers who tend to be content junkies, take King's advice for his own group of content junkies: *"Kill your darlings, kill your darlings, even when it breaks your egocentric little scribbler's heart, kill your darlings."*[28]

Fight against the mentality that all of these beautiful discoveries will truly help your recipients. Much of the golden content that pastors think is essential to their upcoming sermon really isn't needed. These extraneous nuggets may be:

---

[27] Ibid, 226.
[28] Ibid, 222.

- Unaligned with the main idea of the sermon
- Over-explaining a point or idea
- So much detail that it loses our listeners' interest
- Too theologically obtuse for people to grasp
- Simply a bad idea you think is good

Whatever the reason, if those lovely, wonderful, precious nuggets keep the message from maintaining the right pace down the mountain, then be ruthless and kiss those nuggets goodbye!

It is better to preach 70% of what you originally planned for your sermon in order to get 100% effectiveness with your listeners on Sunday, than to preach 100% of what you originally planned but only get 70% effectiveness with your congregants. It's worth repeating: people only get what you give them. When you stand up to preach, the only person who knows you left 30% of your message behind is you! Trust me, the congregation won't feel left out. That is why the biggest hurdle in being ruthlessly simple isn't with your listener nor your material, it's with you.

Frankly, (and this may hurt a little) one's inability to do this with message manuscripts says more about the sermonizer than the sermon. It makes preaching more about the preacher's felt need to say things than the congregants' real need to connect with the things said. Each preacher must remember that the sermon is ultimately for the listener, not the deliverer. Ruthlessness is a wonderful discipline for the preacher because it helps cultivate a heart that loves his listeners more than his sermons. There is a vast difference between loving preaching to people and loving the people to whom you preach. Being ruthless helps give weight to the latter and fights the temptation of the former.

For my fellow content junkies, well-acquainted with the struggle of editing down messages, ask yourself an important question: Does this message really have one path (i.e., one main idea) down the mountain? Based on the amount of content, you might honestly have three distinctive routes in your sermon. Said another way, you have three different messages. This was the case with my friend who I challenged to cut three of his four points – he had four sermons crammed in one message. While on paper it looked great, preaching it would have been less than optimal. The pace would've been too slow and left congregants strewn all across the mountainside due to being lost or bored or, at the very worst, both.

At the conclusion of your sermon preparation, ask yourself, "With this content, am I really preaching one sermon or multiple sermons? What does the path down the mountain really look like with all of this material? What kind of pace is this setting for my listeners?" Better yet, let others look at your manuscript or sermon notes and see what they think about the amount of content. Does your message need to add pace by subtracting material that is unhelpful or too much for one message? There is another aspect of the mountain analogy can help preachers become more ruthlessly simple.

STAYING WITH THE FALL LINE

In skiing there is a concept known as the fall line. It's where you want to keep pointing your skis as you progress down the hill in order to maintain your pace and enjoy the run as it's meant to be. For the preacher, the fall line is the main idea of the message. It's the heart of what you are trying to communicate, giving your listeners the greatest opportunity to think, feel, and/or do what you hoped, by God's grace, the message would accomplish.

THE FALL LINE OF THE MAIN IDEA

MAIN IDEA

A fundamental aspect of preaching well is sticking as closely to your fall line (main idea) as possible. Inversely, the further you "ski" from the fall line by either going off topic or spending too much time in a turn, the greater the risk increases of losing pace and thus, with a thick, tedious message, also losing listeners. Therefore, if the various movements of the sermon don't follow the main idea in a way that carries you and your listeners effectively down the mountain, leave them for another day of skiing.

You can visualize this concept by thinking of out-of-bounds areas on the slope. These are the areas on either side of the run that should be off-limits for the preacher and his eager listeners.

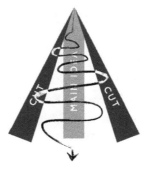

Once you overlay your sermon on the mountain, look where its movements fall on the ski run. How much of the message stays around the fall line of the main idea? Which parts stray too far into the out-of-bounds area? This helps identify turns where there is too much content or the content is off-topic. The out-of-bounds section essentially functions as the "cut section." If sermon elements take you there, they need to either be pared down or removed completely.

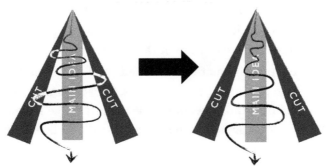

The result of those cuts produces a "tighter" sermon that more closely stays with the main idea, avoiding territory which easily causes listeners to flounder. Each point raised, illustration supplied, or application presented now has the appropriate weight to it. The elements are better fitted to the message. And while your congregants might not be able to articulate the difference, they will definitely sense it.

Staying with the fall line furnishes the message with the speed it demands. It also decreases the likelihood of wondering where all the dynamic in the message (and sanctuary) went on Sunday. But all of it depends on how ruthless the preacher is concerning the sermon's simplicity. Be simple. Be ruthless.

THE AGONY OF DELETE

Great sermons are as much about what you cut as what you keep. Preachers must consistently learn to deal with the agony of delete. I've preached many a sermon where I had to throw out three full pages of sermon manuscript. Was it painful? Absolutely! Did it result in a sermon that will preach better? You bet it did! This is why the end goal isn't putting together a message you personally love, but a message you believe is most effective for those whom you love. That will mean not taking everything from the study with you into the pulpit. Preaching is the art of knowing what to keep and what to cut. Indeed, sometimes the harder determination in sermon preparation isn't what you are going to say but what you are not going to say. And yes, there is always content to delete. It doesn't matter how well-constructed, incredibly insightful, or theologically gripping pastors believe their messages to be – if their people aren't with them at the bottom of the hill, they lose.

At our church, there are times when you'll hear one of us say after preaching the first of three services, "I had too many turns in that message," or "I didn't get down the mountain like I needed to." Truth be told, our preaching team consistently delivers sermons that avoid those troublesome qualities because our preaching DNA is to get down the mountain with the right pace. Using the mountain analogy has helped us consistently produce messages that are built for speed. It forces us to be simple and ruthless. This results in messages with the appropriate pacing to carry the sermon's momentum all the way down the mountain with our people in tow.

CHART
FOR
BANDWIDTH

5
FEELING THROUGH
YOUR SERMON

"I must and will make people listen."
– Charles Haddon Spurgeon

Pastors who have learned to arrange their sermons for tension and build them for speed are making great headway down the path to preaching that moves people by applying the first two letters of the ABC's of preaching. The third and final letter is C – charting the sermon's bandwidth. While it may sound like something hi-tech or sophisticated, it's really quite simple.

Charting the bandwidth of a message involves examining the emotional movement of the sermon. As I mentioned earlier in this book, most preachers scrutinize their sermons for intelligibility or accuracy, wanting each Sunday's message to make sense and faithfully exposit the Scripture. I agree these are indispensable checkpoints for sound preaching. Nevertheless, I would also argue that many well-meaning expositors neglect another important element of the preaching event: *emotional flow*. Put another way, preachers should not just think through their sermons but feel through them as well. We must always ask and answer the question: *What is the emotional flow of my sermon?*

THE IMPORTANCE OF EMOTIONAL FLOW

Every good story – whether it takes the form of a song, show, or book – is deeply cognizant of the emotional dynamic it creates in the recipients. More than simply being aware, these storytellers craft intentional pathways which invoke the sentiments of the reader, listener, or viewer. This purposeful design results in the creation of works that have varied but deliberate emotional flow. Communicators have been thinking this way for millennia.

Do you remember the concept of dramatic structure from your high school English class? I remember learning that Aristotle said every story should have a plot composed of three movements: a beginning, middle, and end.[29] The philosophy of 19th century German playwright and novelist Gustav Freytag expanded on Aristotle's work, giving stories a five-act structure. He popularized what is known as the *dramatic arc. This arc is composed of exposition, rising action, climax, falling action, and dénouement. Each one of these movements is designed not only to impact the* audience intellectually, but to engage them emotionally as well. For example, in the second act of *rising action*, tension builds as events move toward a peak. This device is employed to energize the audience emotionally in order for the story's climax to be satisfying in both head and heart. The hope is that hearers, listeners, or viewers will finish the story having taken a fulfilling journey that unites thoughts and emotions.

Don't lose me here. I'm not arguing that we should arrange sermons according to Aristotle or Freytag, nor am I saying that the aim of our Sunday efforts in the pulpit is the mere tickling of emotions for entertainment's sake. Far from it! Preaching that moves people has nothing to do with the "ear tickling" (cf., 2 Tim.

---

[29] Aristotle called these segments the *protasis, epitasis,* and *catastrophe.*

4:3) of telling people want they want to hear in order for them to feel happy or satisfied. It's not about emotionally manipulating congregants or jettisoning the sound exposition of Scripture in order to create a mood - that is emotionalism, and it's simply wrong.

I'm reminded of Martin Luther's argument concerning the fear of abusing legitimate practices: while it's true that some people abuse their spouses, this is no case for rejecting marriage altogether. In other words, <u>misuse doesn't negate legitimate use</u>. Sometimes I fear that sincere pastors so deeply desire to avoid any semblance of emotional manipulation that they've essentially inoculated their messages from having any real emotional bandwidth. Sermons are given with skin and bone, but no heart. Martin Lloyd-Jones referred to sermons of that ilk as having "light without heat."[30] <u>There is a significant difference between having emotion and emotionalism</u>.

However, I believe that the majority of preachers with little to no emotional bandwidth in their preaching end up there not because they fear the abuse of emotions, but because they don't intentionally consider them at all. The idea of a message's emotional flow just never pops up on the radar of their message prep throughout the week. *Choose sermon text*? Check. *Find main idea*? Check. *Discover illustrations*? Check. *Arrange message for delivery*? Check. *Work through arrangement emotionally to see its flow*? What are you talking about?

Hear me carefully. If one of our objectives as preachers – if not the chief one – is to communicate to our listeners as best we can, then, like communicators from different spheres, we should create messages with the congregants' emotional response in mind. That's the point!

If we can feel through our messages to eliminate elements which could give emotional whiplash to our listeners, why wouldn't we do that? If we can walk through our sermons beforehand and realize our communication doesn't emotionally coincide with our

---

[30] *Preaching and Preachers*, 97.

content, why wouldn't we do that? If we can arrange our content in a way that will help guide congregants emotionally through the message, why wouldn't we do that? I believe that any pastor who desires to emotionally engage his listeners will include efforts like these in his weekly sermon preparation process.

Unfortunately, too many completely miss this way of seeing their sermons. It's evident in the pulpit Sunday after Sunday. These kinds of sermons risk being an exercise not in careful guidance, but in crashing down the mountainside. What's so unnerving about the whole ordeal is the pastor can't understand for the life of him what's going wrong. The message appears sound: points make sense, Scripture is accurately exposited, and both introduction and conclusion feel sound. The preacher believes he's deftly guided his followers around dangerous moguls, down thrilling chutes, and through spine-tingling bends – until he turns around at the bottom of the run to see that hardly anyone is with him.

This disaster is the result of training that only examines sermons structurally but not emotionally. If he had considered how his course through moguls, chutes, and bends might feel to his listeners, he might have realized that the message he had would leave congregants behind all throughout the run. But because our friend didn't intentionally feel his way through the message before preaching it, he lost his congregants during the preaching of it. It is not enough for preachers to think through their messages – they must feel through them as well. Emotional flow matters!

Preachers who desire to preach in a way that moves people should consider employing a simple practice which can assist them in feeling through their messages: charting sermons for bandwidth.

SEEING THE FLOW

Learning to feel through your sermon isn't about manipulating others or putting together a message on the foundation of emotion. Sermons should clearly explain the text in a way that is faithful to the original writing and the centrality of the gospel. But we cannot escape the fact that different elements in our messages will impact the emotions of those who hear it. The job of the preacher is to see that flow and make sure it fits the message and listeners well.

I suggest that pastors take time each week during their sermon preparation to feel through their messages for impact, instead of simply thinking through them for content. Working through a message emotionally helps us see if the progression of sermon movements is coherent, helpful, and thoughtful for the congregation, or if it forces them into emotional whiplashes, flat spots, or dead ends?

Let me illustrate with a message I preached on Hebrews 11:32- 12:2. I was stuck in my sermon preparation. I had tons of ideas dotting my whiteboard but didn't know where to go next. I decided I would work through the flow of the sermon emotionally. I wrote the following:

• The call to faith	**YES!**
• The subtle discouragement	**SIGH.**
• The truth we lose sight of	**HOPE...**
○ The role of Jesus	**REALLY?**
○ The faith of Jesus	
• The grace of the gospel in the faith of Jesus for us	**JOY!**

As you can see, I listed the phrases which summarize each section of the message as it moves from the top of the mountain to the bottom. I then paired them with the emotional responses I believe the majority of my hearers will exhibit. As to whether or not congregants will actually feel these emotions in the preaching event, I can't be completely sure. But considering which emotions will arise from these sermon segments enables me to craft the message in a way that makes better sense emotionally, not just cognitively. I can select illustrations, stories, and other elements that align with the emotional flow to more effectively guide the congregation to the base of the mountain.

In this message, I was hoping those listening to my exposition of Hebrews 11:32-12:2 would move from initial exuberance, to mild frustration, to a blossoming hope, to an "Aha" moment that finds its conclusion in a joy only tethered to the gospel of Jesus. I certainly couldn't guarantee that it would work just like that. The Holy Spirit always has the final say. But taking time to intentionally think about my message's emotional flow not only has rescued me from being stuck in the sermon prep process but also has taught me to see my sermons differently – to actually *feel* through them.

I challenge you to try the same. On a whiteboard or sheet of paper, write out the major movements of your message, then pair each section with what you imagine will be your listener's emotional response. If it helps, think about what type of emoji you would place next to each. Does this cause people to respond in joy, sorrow, questioning, so something else? The point of this exercise is to increase your capacity to decipher your sermons emotionally.

THE EMOTIONAL CENTER

Learning to feel through sermons will not only prepare pastors for the next step of charting them for bandwidth but will tutor them in distinguishing a sermon's emotional center as well. The emotional center of a message is that moment when listeners; hearts connect with the main idea of the message. Instead of simply connecting in the listener's head, the emotional center gives the sermon cohesion in the heart. From the preacher's point of view, it's what makes the message *feel* like a message, rather than a lecture.

Art like songs, stories, and shows appeal to their recipients because something strikes their feelings, not just their intellect. While a sermon must do more than simply touch the emotions of those who listen, it should not do less. Preachers who want to move people in their preaching must simultaneously aim at two targets:

head *and* heart. Sermonizers must instruct congregants in the truth and put before them the emotions that faithfully and properly flow from the truth.

Discerning a sermon's emotional center is to investigate what unites the message emotionally. It's the dominant or primary emotional element that flows from the truths presented in the sermon. Sermons without an emotional center will come across as dry, dispassionate, and distant. I have preached more than my share of those kinds of sermons. While every element in the message had its place in my manuscript, I could not have told you where the "heart" of the sermon was. I would not have been able to demonstrate where the people (or even I) would emotionally connect in the message most deeply.

Often the emotional center is found where the preacher himself is most moved by the message. It's that place in the sermon where every time he talks through his message notes, it makes his heart race, his eyes moisten, or his brow furrow. The emotional center may make him weepy, exhilarated, or intense – but no matter what the response, it's the place where he responds with his heart and not merely his head. And if it moves him, it will likely be that part of the message with which his listeners most deeply connect.

Don't preach a sermon where you can't identify the location of its emotional center, because it might mean there isn't one. Go back to your study and apply what you learned in this chapter. Feel through your sermon! Trace the emotional flow of the message, looking for any dissonance or gaps. You may discover that you have built a "Tin Man" message with wonderful structure, strategic movements, and insightful points, but sadly, no heart. It does not guide the congregation anywhere emotionally because it has no emotional center. Developing your ability to feel through your messages may mean the difference between giving lectures and preaching sermons.

This leads us to the next phase of feeling through our sermons. Once we begin to think emotionally about our messages and their emotional center, we are ready to actually chart them for bandwidth.

6

CHART FOR BANDWIDTH

"Many a preacher misses the mark because,
though he knows books, he does not know men."
— JAMES STALKER

O nce pastors grow more adept at feeling through their sermons, they can take the next step by charting sermons for bandwidth. This visualization of the emotional entirety of their sermons will help them better discern a message's emotional flow. Engaging in this exercise can be eye-opening for those who struggle in the pulpit to connect emotionally with their congregants.

Start by drawing three lines and labelling them as follows:

HIGH
━━━━━━━━━━━━━━━━━━━━━━━━━━━━━━━━━

■ ━ ■ ━ ■ ━ ■ STASIS ■ ━ ■ ━ ■ ━ ■

━━━━━━━━━━━━━━━━━━━━━━━━━━━━━━━━━
LOW

Think of this chart as akin to those used by musicians. Higher marks signify higher emotional "notes" of the perceived response to the message (e.g., exhilaration, joy, etc.). The same holds true respectively for the middle and bottom of the chart. You will use this device to plot the message's *highs*, *lows*, and *stasis*. I define stasis as the emotional middle within an individual's sermon – being neither up nor down emotionally. Stasis is the emotional baseline that is the reference point for the sermon's highs and lows. You can also add divisions of introduction and conclusion to help you visualize the sermon's bandwidth as it works its way through the message.

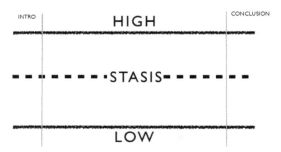

Once the boundary markers have been set out, we can begin to chart the emotional flow of the sermon. How would you draw out the emotional high, lows, and midst of the last message you preached? Think about the emotional response you believe congregants will display in relation to the content they hear. One example might look like this:

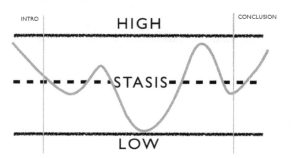

Here we have a message whose takeoff is emotionally "up." It could be something very humorous or seriously intense. Once the introduction gives way to the body of the message, we see the sermon move into more conversational tones that stay within a neutral or middle ground emotionally. Then, towards the halfway point of the message, the sermon goes "down" emotionally. This doesn't mean the preacher has become depressed, but the message content has brought the congregants to a lower emotional response. This could be a touching story about someone's struggle with a terminal illness or the disclosure of personal suffering. It could even be the pastor calling out sin which might evoke quiet conviction amongst the congregants.

We can also note on this specific chart that the sermon begins to work its way up towards the message's conclusion. There is a "coming up for air" or moment of emotional relief in the message as we see the sermon line reaches the stasis marker. Maybe the preacher said something appropriately humorous, or he pastorally guided congregants through their emotional issues after giving them some tough words to digest. Whatever he said, the preacher took his listeners toward an emotional equilibrium that allowed them to appropriately move toward a high part of the message. Hopefully this example helps you better understand how our team sees a message that's been charted for bandwidth. The goal is to identify and evaluate the sermon's emotional movements from start to finish.

CHARTING DIFFERENT TYPES OF SERMONS

I haven't met many preachers who actually feel through their sermons before preaching them. But to me it makes all the difference. Charting for bandwidth allows us to feel through our message in a way that gives us the ability to see potential problems with how our content is presented to congregants. For instance, it may reveal that we have arranged a sermon in an emotionally unhelpful fashion. Here are examples of charts which reveal problems in a message's emotional flow.

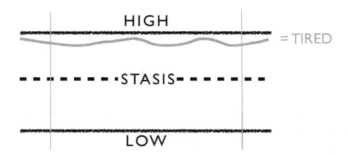

This chart depicts a pastor who might be treating his sermon as a pep rally that never ends. He might be speaking in a raised voice from start to finish or be so excited that he never finds any space in the journey to calm down. He never sees the need for emotional deceleration. This type of message leaves congregants feeling like they've run a marathon. They're exhausted because the sermon gave them no place to emotionally catch their breath. After it's over, men and women gratefully drag themselves out of the sanctuary yearning for the solitude of getting into a quiet car.

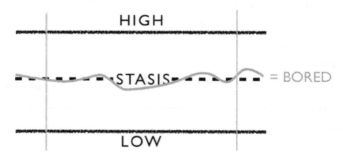

This chart is what I like to call the "Bueller" sermon because it reminds me of the iconic scene in the movie *Ferris Bueller's Day Off* where Ben Stein plays the emotionally-bereft economics teacher who repeatedly utters Ferris' last name during roll call, all with the enthusiasm of a dead animal.[31] He then proceeds to teach the class with the same 'just-barely-alive' emotional tone.

---

[31] Why is Ferris absent? Well, the rumor from someone's best friend's sister's boyfriend's brother's girlfriend heard from this guy who knows this kid who's going with the girl who saw Ferris passed out at 31 Flavors the night before. Everyone guesses it's pretty serious.

The result is a slow death for the students. The camera shows their deer-in-the-headlights faces with mouths agape and eyes plastered over, as Stein's character begs for engagement with his emotionless invitation: *Anyone? Anyone?* (You can hear him, can't you?) It's an iconic scene because of the humor it evokes in watching a robotic-like teacher who is completely unaware of the emotional temperature around him, yet continues to communicate in a way that is the opposite of life-giving.

The "Bueller" sermon is really a bad lecture in disguise. The pastor hovers around the midline, where everything has the same compact emotional tone. The sermon's happy, sad, or exciting elements feel too closely tethered to the middle, never given the appropriate emotional resonance they deserve. Nothing really feels up or down. This narrow bandwidth is a recipe for a bored congregation. Congregants may start to think, "Does this guy really believe what he's saying or not?" because he sounds the same way about everything. This type of message often leaves a huge emotional disconnect with listeners.

While the sermon might have a generally pleasant feel to it, it's the feeling one gets listening to elevator music. The tone is okay for moments here and there, but as in Bueller's economics class, a constant midline mood can feel like a slide into oblivion. Don't let your sermons bore your congregants to death. It's an affront to both the call of preaching and the glory of the gospel.

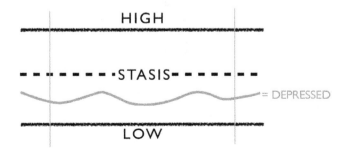

This is what I call the "Eeyore" sermon. Surely you remember the dear but downcast A.A. Milne character from the beloved *Winnie-the-Pooh* series? For this cherished donkey, nothing is worth celebrating; on the contrary, all is doom and gloom. Eeyore makes us believe that he would look on the bright side, if he could find it. To be around him is to experience a continually low bandwidth of emotion that possesses the supernatural ability to depress those with even the cheeriest of dispositions.

This is the kind of message where the pastor strings together emotionally-draining elements back-to-back-to-back in the sermon without ever "coming up for air" (i.e., moving toward the stasis midline). It's not just using a story of injustice in the message, but how angered the pastor is by no one in the congregation doing anything about it – he even feels the need to spend the rest of the message making sure that specific conviction (or rather, guilt) sets in on his listeners. Or maybe it's the message that deals with a national crisis by continually pointing to how bad things are in our country, using sobering illustration after sobering illustration without ever really moving toward hope. Even if there is a glimmer of respite, it's so brief toward the end of the message that congregants weren't in the right emotional place to make use of it.

The Eeyore sermon is guaranteed to depress listeners. Some congregants will leave on Sunday wondering how this whole Christianity-thing can actually be thought of as good news. It's just one more example why pastors should more intentionally consider their sermon's emotional flow.

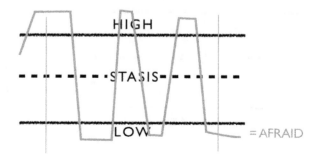

Frankly, this is the kind of message whose emotional flow leaves the congregants wondering if there is something seriously wrong with the preacher. The erratic jumps from low to high and high to low cause listeners to not only be afraid for themselves but the pastor as well, unsure if he's emotionally stable. Consequently, there's usually a quick exit toward the doors once the service is over. While this example is given a little tongue-in-cheek, there are sermons which can nearly imitate this chart in spirit due to the preacher's lack of emotional IQ.

This type of sermon is not only hard to follow but leaves people very confused, if not a little apprehensive, as the message flies through emotional ups and downs with no logical reason for the abrupt shifts. *Why did Pastor Joe tell a joke right before sharing the story of a couple's struggle with infertility?* Congregants suffer emotional whiplash as the sermon "strips the gears" moving from high to low and back again, with little sympathy for the listeners' ability to emotionally process what they're hearing. This is where the midline becomes the pastor's friend. Stasis smooths emotional transitions and allows breathing room for your listeners to work through the emotional peaks and valleys of your sermon.

All these examples stress the importance of preachers charting their message's emotional bandwidth. Does this mean every preacher needs to do this practice? No. There are many expositors gifted with a naturally expansive bandwidth in their preaching. They effortlessly move through the highs and lows of a sermon and guide their congregation's journey through those elements with relative ease. However, it seems that for every preacher who can do this well, there are ten who cannot.

NOT ALL MESSAGES ARE THE SAME

While the majority of sermons need some kind of combination of high, lows, and mids, it would do us well to understand that, when charted for bandwidth, messages are not supposed to look the same.[32] You can have generally high or "up" sermons as well as predominately low or "down" messages. One sermon might be more emotionally-charged while another might have a largely somber timber to it. Yet every sermon, regardless of its general tenor, will need some fluctuation in emotional bandwidth.

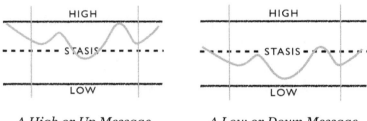

A High or Up Message   A Low or Down Message

As already mentioned, high or emotionally-charged messages will need to come down at times in order for people to catch their breath, just as a chiefly "down" or somber message should allow moments for congregants to come up for air. This is why the stasis level is important to keep in mind while charting your bandwidth. It brings listeners relief from emotional highs and lows, allowing them to better connect for the full duration of the message, rather than leaving them stuck at one emotional level.

Charting for bandwidth is additionally helpful because it gets pastors outside themselves in the sermon preparation process. Far too often preachers put together messages with arrangements they intuitively believe work best. While intuition is helpful, it can often lead us astray. Charting a message's emotional flow enables the pastor to move from his all-too-often myopic perspective on the message to a constructive distance where he can be more objective about the effectiveness of the message's arrangement.

Charting leads preachers to see areas of need in the sermon they

---

[32] For example, sermons which seek to exposit large amounts of Scripture will likely have long stretches of bandwidth that mirror the emotional tenor and flow of the text it seeks to exposit.

were unable to identify before. For example, the message may begin too high emotionally for the subject matter, meaning the introduction will need to be tweaked or completely replaced. The sermon may spend too long in stasis, leaving dead spots within the message. Using the skiing analogy, it's equivalent to the drudgery of having to pole over flat ground. A pastor also might recognize that the sermon's conclusion should move higher emotionally in order to allow congregants to soak in what was said. Each of these insights can be products of charting the message's emotional bandwidth, because it allows pastors the perspective of distance they might not otherwise have.

One of the things I hear most from those who chart their sermons' bandwidth is how dramatically it has improved the preaching experience. They feel a greater seamlessness in the sermon's execution. The message elements seem to progress with more emotional intentionality, and the majority of the congregation appears to stay with the sermon to the end.

Another benefit for those who consistently chart their bandwidth is increasing their intuitive sense of the message's emotional flow. Some pastors told me they have become so adept at feeling through their messages via charting that they only do so now when the sermon deals with an especially sensitive topic, where getting the right emotional tone is absolutely paramount. Developing that skill alone is reason enough to consider charting your sermons for emotional bandwidth.

SMALLER-BANDWIDTH PREACHERS

As mentioned in the introduction, Phillips Brooks defined preaching as "truth communicated through personality." Each preacher has a specific emotional dynamic he brings into the pulpit, and the scale of that dynamic will look different for each person. There are preachers who, by personality, are more extroverted, while others are more introverted. Consequently, some who alight the pulpit on Sundays will have a naturally larger emotional zone available to them (e.g., my friend Matt Chandler), and others will have a naturally smaller zone to work with (e.g., my wannabe friend Tim Keller). When charting bandwidth, pastors should scale their charts to fit their personalities.

However, it's not too uncommon for those who begin charting their sermons to grow a little disappointed by the realization that they are small-bandwidth preachers. Because of their personality, they have a naturally limited or smaller emotional dynamic. These preachers don't raise their voices, get choked up, or become physically animated in the pulpit. They are simply more reserved in personality. To take upon themselves the vocal or physical habits of more emotionally dynamic preachers would be an exercise in falsehood. It's just not how God wired them.

After talking about the importance of a sermon's emotional flow, I often get asked, "Yancey, I'm a fairly reserved guy in the pulpit. What am I supposed to do?"

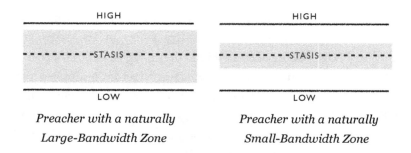

Preacher with a naturally   *Preacher with a naturally*
Large-Bandwidth Zone   *Small-Bandwidth Zone*

While I will address this more in-depth later in the book, I first want to reassure them that, no matter what, they should be themselves in the pulpit. Naturally limited-bandwidth preachers attempting to employ the behaviors of those with naturally large emotional bandwidths is almost always a recipe for disaster. It will ruin them in the long run and their congregations as well. The temptation however is real. No one wants to feel like they preach boring messages. While we can talk about the power of content all we want, there is a reality behind delivery we cannot avoid. Many of those with smaller emotional bandwidths fear preaching "un-dynamic" messages that lull congregations to sleep. Though smaller-bandwidth preachers should never apishly mimic the preaching style of larger-bandwidth preachers, they can focus instead on properly filling the bandwidth they naturally have.

For example, both Fig. 1 and Fig. 2 describe the same preacher who has a naturally smaller emotional bandwidth.

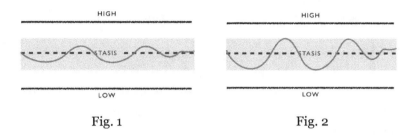

Fig. 1   Fig. 2

The grey area is the zone of the preacher's emotional bandwidth, showing the limits of how emotionally high or low he can authentically reach. Fig. 1 shows a sermon where the pastor isn't maximizing the limited bandwidth he possesses. This results in a sermon which comes across emotionally flat and probably boring. The truth is, even though the preacher has a smaller emotional bandwidth, he can still expand it (Fig. 2). He can go higher and lower emotionally and continue to be himself. He can still remain natural. He doesn't need to engage in histrionics or succumb to the temptation of plug-and-playing someone else's personality. Both are kisses of death for the preacher in the long run.

INCREASING YOUR BANDWIDTH

There are other ways of increasing the dynamic for those with a naturally smaller emotional zone. It must be noted that these methods can become unhelpful crutches if used in place of the hard work of sermon crafting. The key is employing them in a way that honors the integrity of the sermon, not subverting it. With that said, if you have a smaller emotional range as a preacher, consider increasing your bandwidth by *appropriately* implementing these elements:

- Stories/Illustrations
- Images/Videos
- Props
- Wordcrafting – painting pictures with words
- Dialogue/Interview
- Self-disclosure
- Pace – rate of speech (both faster and slower)

As you may notice, many of these elements are tied to creativity. Creativity is a friend to preachers with naturally smaller emotional zones. But creativity has a dark side as well. If used as the meat instead of simply the dressing, creativity becomes counterproductive. Our charge is to preach the Word, not sidestep it by an over-reliance on creative elements. That is gimmick-driven preaching, not gospel-driven preaching. However, if used wisely, creativity can be a good way to widen one's emotional bandwidth.

One last way to ensure that you're preaching within your full emotional range is to evaluate your passion. Nothing impacts the bandwidth of a sermon more than the sermonizer's intensity in the message. I tell our preachers at Clear Creek Community Church: *If there is only one person in the room who believes what you're saying, let it be you!* In other words, preach with conviction. Let your proclamation from the pulpit be weighted down with the burden that you have truth worth hearing and, better yet, worth receiving and living. A preacher's personal belief in the truth of his sermon can generate enough bandwidth in and of itself. Comprehension is good, but conviction is better.

AIM AT HEADS AND HEARTS

Bandwidth is an oft-forgotten but important aspect of great preaching. Personally, I didn't hear much of anything about the emotional aspect of a sermon in my training as a preacher. Yet over my more than two decades of preaching, I've seen that understanding the importance of a sermon's emotional flow is invaluable. Preaching messages with a smarter emotional bandwidth often leads to sermons which are more apt to move congregants, because we've intentionally sought to guide our hearers through those messages both intellectually and emotionally. We've aimed at heads and hearts. May we be preachers who not only think through our sermons but feel through them as well.

7

BEFORE THE PLUNGE

"All you have to do is go that way...really fast.
If something gets in your way, turn."
– Better Off Dead

I n the 80's teen comedy movie, *Better Off Dead,* teenager Lane
Myers and his French foreign-exchange student friend,
Monique, stand on the top of a mountain at the edge of K-12, a
ski run of legendary difficulty. Petrified at the sight of the imposing
trail, Lane squeaks, "Look at this! How am I supposed to live
through this?" Monique responds, "All you have to do is go that
way...really fast. If something gets in your way, turn." She then
proceeds to effortlessly ski the K-12. At the bottom, Monique
encourages her friend that it's his turn. Seeing how easy the run was
for his female friend, Lane confidently takes the plunge over the
edge. Immediately things go awry. Lane falls from the start,
shouting in pain as he tumbles through the entire run.

If a sermon is like taking a group of fellow skiers on a wondrous,
exhilarating journey down a mountain, then this chapter is
dedicated to those moments that conclude with you on Sunday
morning gazing over your ski tips as they dangle over the edge of a
run. All that's left is to take the plunge. The question is: have you
done the necessary work to ensure this will be a journey worth

taking, or will you wind up like Lane?

Many a preacher has stood behind a pulpit thinking himself ready to point his skis downhill and take his congregants on a great journey, only to experience a run full of falls. Let me share some areas to think through, like a pre-run checklist, so that when you take the plunge Sunday morning, you'll do so knowing you've prepared as best you can to take your congregation on an exciting journey down the mountain.

MAKE SURE IT'S GOOD MORE THAN ONCE

Whenever the message manuscript/outline/Post-it Note is completed, pastors may tend to assume that their message is ready to preach merely because it feels good at that moment – all that's left to do is wait for Sunday. However, there are more checkpoints to consider. Let me encourage you to work through specific iterations of the message throughout the week, with the goal of giving the green light to your message at each stage – more places where you can say, "This is good." Consider implementing these five stages, or checkpoints, as quality control for your message's readiness to plunge down the mountain:

STAGE #1: PITCH IT

Give a five-minute thumbnail sketch to a staff member, friend, or spouse of your message's path down the mountain. I call it a "pitch" because you essentially say, "Hey, do you have five minutes? Here's what I'm thinking for Sunday." Then you proceed to succinctly describe the message's idea and flow as best as you presently know it. While it might be difficult this early in the process to spot how good the message is at this juncture, rest assured that bad ideas and movements can be seen by others at this stage. Their reflections about your admittedly half-baked elements can be the difference between starting strong or stumbling out of the blocks in sermon preparation. This benefit alone demonstrates the value of pitching your sermon first.

STAGE #2: WRITE IT

This is the stage where you finish your notes for Sunday.[33] You think it's good because you've done the hard work throughout the week, it's fresh on your mind, and, frankly, because you think you are finally done with it. But you're not done yet.

STAGE #3: READ IT

The most beneficial thing I do once my initial notes are completed is take a red marker and read through each page of my manuscript. I'm amazed (as well as discouraged) how reading through my message allows me to catch unhelpful digressions, misaligned ideas, fuzzy illustrations, and other elements of the message that need retracting, adding, or moving. It also gives me better perspective to see how closely I'm following the sermon's fall line. An edited message is the recipe for a stronger message. Afterward, I can hardly believe that I was going to stand in front of people and preach without those changes. But once again, there is still more to be done.

STAGE #4: TALK IT

A great manuscript does not equal a great message. Preaching is an oral medium, so talking through your message out loud can be incredibly beneficial. You may find that what works on paper doesn't work in the pulpit. In almost every sermon manuscript I talk through, I discover statements or sections that need to be rewritten for the spoken word. Once you feel confident about the message after talking it out, you might think it's good to go. But there's still one more stage.

STAGE #5 PREACH IT

There is a dynamic in preaching itself that cannot be duplicated in talking through your message alone. There are times in preaching where you see certain elements of your message that connect with

---

[33] I will argue for manuscripting during this stage later in the chapter.

your congregants better than others. There are also moments where you say things extemporaneously that the Holy Spirit uses in great ways. You may think: *Man, I wish I had written that down.* Do so! After the service, jot down those thoughts, phrases, and illustrations into your notes. Personally, it's in the preaching event where I frequently say unscripted things to give a better flow to my message or further explain certain elements. If that happens to you, just know they might be gold.[34] Don't throw them away. Capture them. Write them down. Continue editing your message by deleting parts you believe aren't helpful or expanding sections that are.

This is obviously beneficial for pastors who preach multiple services, but it's also a plus if you have the opportunity to give that message again in the future. Either way, the preaching event itself is the final checkpoint for knowing when a sermon is really good or not. As disheartening as that may sound, sometimes you just don't know how good a message really is until you actually preach it. So:

PITCH it.
WRITE it.
READ it.
TALK it.
PREACH it.

Regardless of one's approach to sermon preparation, don't give yourself only one place in the process to evaluate whether or not the message is ready for Sunday. Create several opportunities before getting into the pulpit (and even after it). You may realize the message wasn't as good as you originally thought. It could be better – much better! That's why you give yourself the opportunity to edit at every stage. Installing a process with various checkpoints grants preachers some measure of confidence that, while the Lord must

---

[34] I recognize these extemporaneous offerings could also be the product of undisciplined thought and long-windedness, which all the more highlights the need for others to help you evaluate the preaching event.

BEFORE THE PLUNGE 113

grant his grace in the preaching event, you have a mountain of a message that merits taking a plunge.

A WORD ABOUT MANUSCRIPTING

Years back I pulled a Bible from my shelf that was given to me by my father during my first semester of college. In it I found several old sermon outlines that I preached during my time in school. I was immediately struck by the difference between those old sermon notes and the ones I use today. My old notes were handwritten, one-page outlines that mostly consisted of phrases, alliterated points, and Scripture references. There wasn't one complete paragraph I could find in any of them. Illustrations were simply noted by the letter "I" with a circle around it, followed by a word or two (e.g., man with dog, broken bicycle). This epitomized my sermon preparation. I would study, take mental notes, scratch a few things out here and there on a scrap of paper, then proceed to write a sermon outline from which to preach. I continued this simple process through seminary, my first full-time position, and in the initial years at my current church. If memory serves me correctly, I preached my first sermon at Clear Creek Community Church from something akin to a 5×7 note card on which was written a rather scant outline.

It was a good process. It was efficient (I don't like to over-prepare). It fit my preaching style (I am an extemporaneous preacher). I felt it would serve me well for the long-haul, yet today I employ a preparation process whereby I manuscript the entire message, though I still preach from an outline. Why the change? Initially, it's because I admired the preaching of my senior pastor. He manuscripted his messages and would preach the lights out. I thought I could possibly get better as a preacher by doing the same. Today, I see at least three reasons why I like manuscripting messages in the sermon prep process while still preaching from an outline.

First, manuscripting refines my thinking. In the editing process, I'm better able to see how different sections interact with each other. *Does my illustration really support what I've just said? Is this the best place for it in my message? Am I saying too much here or not enough?* You may be able to do this to some degree with a generalized outline; however, a manuscript affords me greater clarity about my thought process in putting a sermon together. I don't have to debate what I'm thinking at each point in the message – the manuscript shows me what I'm thinking. In fact, it does so in great detail, in addition to what changes need to be made.

Second, manuscripting sharpens my speaking. What you hear in your head as you read your notes (READ it) can be very different once you speak through your sermon (TALK it). Speaking through my message helps me see where different elements of it may be too chunky or too thin or just right. A manuscript allows me to work as closely as possible to the message that actually gets preached on Sunday. I can hear in detail, for example, how a phrase sounds. *Can it be rewritten for greater effectiveness? Is this the best way to communicate what I need to say? Are there more memorable ways of saying this?* I also find manuscripting keeps me from rambling, chasing unhelpful rabbits, or being incoherent in the pulpit. Honestly, it helps me from being lazy. I can't say, "Well, I'll just figure out how to say that on Sunday."

Finally, manuscripting is better stewardship. In my early years, being invited to speak at other churches was always an exercise in frustration. I would pull out my sermon notes which, because they were in sparse outline form, were essentially unpreachable. I would read something like "Illustration: Man with Dog." That was it. What was I supposed to do with that? Manuscripting filled in the blanks, taking out the guesswork and blank stares that went with my meager sermon outlines. It made me a good steward of all the hard work I'd put into preaching. Manuscripting allowed me to not only re-preach messages but also use that content in future endeavors (e.g., training material, seminars, etc.).

Once again, I don't preach from a manuscript. I don't bring one into the pulpit. I do take a really big outline with me. I'm still a rather extemporaneous speaker. More often than not I prefer flow over precision (think: *Get down the mountain!*). But while it's more time-consuming, using a manuscript in the sermon prep process has also been more rewarding. Try it. See if it refines your thinking, sharpens your speaking, and is better prepares you for the plunge on Sunday.

FIND YOUR SERMON LENGTH SWEET SPOT

Debates have occurred amongst preachers as to what is the best length for a sermon. I've heard it all. There are those who vouch for sermon lengths of 45 minutes to an hour (or longer), warning that "sermonettes make Christianettes." Others take their cues from the TED Talk philosophy, saying 18 minutes or so is more than enough time for any good communicator to get the message across. Personally, based on what I believe about the demands of biblical exposition, it would be tough to accomplish what needs to be done if given only eighteen minutes. However, I also think 45 minutes is probably too much time for most preachers. Yet with that being said, I believe sermon length isn't something to be dogmatic about. The reality is that every congregation retains a receptivity threshold for the length of sermons. If pastors regularly exceed that threshold, they are more apt to lose their hearers' attention, patience, and sometimes attendance. Sermons with length problems become self-defeating because they accomplish the opposite of what pastors intend for their congregants.

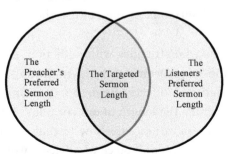

Every pastor has a sweet spot for the sermon length he believes is effective for him. For me, it's around 35 minutes. The congregation also has a sweet spot for the duration of listening. Too short of a sermon and they feel like they're getting cheated; too long a message and they check out. Pastors who care about preaching in a way that moves people will try to find common ground between their sweet spot and their congregation's sweet spot. If they share the same time, then it's a match made in heaven. Congratulations, you won the preaching lottery! If not, I would counsel pastors to move towards their congregation's threshold. Unfortunately, in my experience, pastors typically expect congregants to do the moving.

I hear all kinds of rationale for letting the church serve the pastor in this area instead of the other way around.

- *I just can't preach the whole Word of God unless I go 50 minutes.*
- *My elders refuse to let me trim 10 minutes from my sermons.*
- *It's just hard to be me unless I've got an entire hour.*

Many pastors don't think about sermon length because of the generally positive reflection they receive from their parishioners about their preaching. However, the reason for that could be because most of the men and women who fill the pews on Sunday are too kind to say anything they feel might hurt the feelings of their pastor. But when his stand-in's supply messages that are five to ten minutes shorter, they will make half-hearted jokes about their pastor's long-winded sermons as they praise the guest preacher's message.

Like anyone else who struggles with addiction, part of getting help with way-too-long-sermonizing is admitting one has a problem. Congregational effectiveness, not personal emotional fulfillment, should guide the length of our sermons. If that's where you want to be, but you're not sure how to make strides toward shorter sermons, here's the one piece of advice I would give: *Get comfortable with being uncomfortable.*

There is no way around it. You will be frustrated with giving shorter messages. You will feel they are incomplete and bare. If you're used to 45-minute messages, you'll feel like 35 minutes is giving devotions instead of sermons. You will have to battle thinking that you're some kind of spiritual sellout because you trimmed 10 minutes off your hour-long message. But know this – the learning curve for getting comfortable with preaching shorter sermons won't be with your congregants, only with you. Get comfortable with being uncomfortable because moving toward the common ground where your sweet spot for preaching and their sweet spot for listening meet can really be hard on the preacher. You will need to remind yourself: it is better to have a 35-minute message that moves people and frustrates you than a 45-minute message that moves you but frustrates them.

Don't compare the length of your sermons with those preached by others. Remember, you are not them. They are not you. Don't believe the myth that preaching longer sermons means you're somehow a better preacher. It's not true. You may just be a long-winded, mentally unorganized, travel all over the mountain preacher. It is reported that William Jennings Bryan's mother, after hearing him speak, remarked to her orator son, "You missed several good opportunities to sit down." Don't let that be said about your preaching.

If all this comes across to you with the tone of some biblical rebuke, rest easy. Reducing the sermon length to more effectively interface with your congregation's receptivity bandwidth doesn't equate to Paul's admonition in 2 Timothy 4:3 about false teachers who appease their congregants' "itching ears." Paul doesn't speak against preaching *shorter* sermons, but *unsound* ones. There are pastors around the globe whose hour-plus sermons would qualify as the unsound teaching found in 2 Tim. 4:3. Don't be bullied into thinking sermon length equates to spiritual maturity or giving your folk "meat," where longer means better. If you want to get down the mountain well, before you even take the plunge, make sure you've got a message whose length stands on the common ground between your sweet spot for message length and the congregation's sweet spot for hearing that message.

DRAW A LINE EARLIER IN YOUR WEEK

Saturday Night Special. Gun enthusiasts understand this as any kind of cheap handgun. Others know it as a song from the 70's Southern rock band Lynyrd Skynyrd. Preachers employ this term for messages written the night before a Sunday morning service. Most pastors I speak with don't begin and end their sermon writing on Saturday, but many work on their messages all the way up to Saturday night.[35] I don't. My routine is to write the guts of my message by Tuesday and finish it by noon Wednesday. I then edit down my manuscript to a preaching outline on Thursday morning. That's it. I don't even see or think about my sermon until I read it aloud (i.e., the "TALK it" stage) Saturday night. I intentionally shifted my message prep to terminate earlier rather than later in the week by drawing a line in my schedule where I committed not to work anymore on my sermon. While not wanting this to come across as a law every preacher must observe, I would offer three reasons for its consideration.

The first is that drawing a line in your week puts the right hours on the right things. Many preachers think they need time later in the week to fine-tune their message in order to improve the sermon from, say, a grade of 80 to a 90. But in all likelihood, those extra hours only enhance the message from 80 to an 82. When you consider the amount of time invested in the second half of the week for sermon prep, including Saturday, it's just not worth it. The return on investment is too little. There are other pastoral items in

---

[35] Spurgeon's regular practice was to finish arranging his sermon outline on Saturday night. (http://archive.spurgeon.org/misc/amm05.php; accessed August 12, 2017). This is also the practice of modern-day preachers like Mark Dever. Russell Moore has written that he finalizes his messages early Sunday morning. (http://news.sbts.edu/2009/08/27/prepare-to-preach-both-heart-and-mind-must-be-made-ready-say-sbts-profpastors/; accessed August 12, 2017)

your schedule which need that precious time. Drawing a line in your week acts as a guardrail – allowing you to steward your time for the rest of your calling, not only as a preacher but a leader. Put the right hours on the right things!

QUESTION:
What hours are you giving your sermon that you should be giving to something else in your church?

Drawing a line in your week also makes a statement about your priorities outside of preaching and pastoral ministry. It makes you available to other important spheres of your life like your family. When I was younger, I spent many evenings at home working on my messages. I'd come home, dine with my wife and kids, and then go off in a room to study while my family tried to be a family without me. It was a net loss for the week. Today, I intentionally don't spend evenings or weekends with my sermon. I spend them with my family. Finishing my sermon earlier in the week made a statement to my wife and children that they also are a priority in my life. Making myself available to my sermon at the beginning of the week enabled me to make myself available to my family at the end of the week. Our Saturday nights are special!

And when I'm with my family, I'm truly *with* them. I'm not thinking about illustrations when I see my kid pitch at his Little League game. I don't wonder how I'll intro my message when I'm out to eat with my wife. I'm fully present wherever I am with them. Drawing a line in my week makes a clear statement that I value my life as a husband, father, and friend as much as I value my life as a preacher.

QUESTION:
What does your current sermon preparation routine say about how you prioritize your other values?

Drawing a line in your week frees you up to work on the *how* of your sermon. As I stated at the beginning of this book, preachers too frequently work on the *what* of their sermon at the expense of the *how*. They give hours, if not days, to developing content for a message, while devoting mere minutes to the delivery of that content. But drawing a line in your week can encourage you to give at least some thought to your sermon's delivery, creating space for the "READ it" and "TALK it" stages. If, for example, your line is Wednesday at noon for the sermon's *what*, you still have quite a bit of time (without running into the weekend) to think through the sermon's *how*.

QUESTION:

How much of your weekly sermon preparation is focused on your delivery?

Give it a try. Draw a line in your week. Tell yourself that the sermon creation, for all intents and purposes, is done when you get to that line. You'll be tempted to blow past it with rationalizations and excuses ad infinitum. But for your sake, your family's sake, and your church's sake, consider drawing a line in your week and sticking to it. Let Saturday Night Specials be the rare exception instead of the norm. You'll be better for it when you step to the edge before taking the plunge, and so will your family and church.

CONSIDER STUDYING LESS

One of the reasons some pastors are unwilling to draw a line earlier in their week is because of the sheer number of hours they put in the study. It's nothing for them to drop 25 to 30 hours a week per message. As heretical as it sounds, I want to encourage those pastors to study less. Let me qualify that statement. You might skip this advice if:

*

- Your sermon prep is less than 10 hours a week.
- Your job only requires you to preach and nothing else.
- You're less than five years into your preaching ministry.

But if you spend a big percentage of your week on sermon prep (20 to 25 hours) and actually have other things that need your attention as a pastor, father, husband, friend, or any other roles you play, I want to challenge you to reduce the amount of time you spend in the study.

Many preachers think the pulpit would suffer greatly if they don't put in, for example, 25 hours' worth of work on their sermon each week. While that might feel true in the mind of the preacher, it isn't in the minds of his congregants. In other words, it's a myth to think that strategically reducing the number of hours studying would completely shipwreck the effectiveness of your message on Sunday. To be clear, I am not advocating one's sermon preparation time go from 25 hours a week to two. I am recommending preachers think strategically about cutting an appropriate chunk of time from their study, in order that those hours be better utilized.

For example, I recently recommended a preacher who studied about 25 hours a week to reduce his study time to 15 hours. Think about the implications of that commitment. Imagine how much a person could do with 10 more hours a week. As I noted earlier, someone might free up 10 hours to give to his wife and kids each week or reallocate some of those hours for strategic issues the church is facing. What would you do with those hours? Do you think it would enhance areas of your life and ministry that could use that extra time? I want to be clear – this isn't a call to preach poor sermons because one isn't giving the necessary time message preparation demands, but rather being open to the possibility that those sermons would retain their effectiveness for the listener even with a reasonable reduction of one's time in the study. And, as a result, other important spheres of your life would be greatly enhanced.

Sermon preparation is like a sponge. Your message under construction will reach a saturation point during the week where its increase in effectiveness becomes incremental instead of monumental. The wise preacher must discern the time where worthwhile change begins to be imperceptible and let that drive the quest to find the right amount of study time. What's your message's saturation point? When would adding more hours only get your message miniscule improvements? Not only is that your target time for study, but I'd argue it's likely several hours less than you currently give each week. Again, it's not that the hours-past-saturation are wasted, it's just that they could be better maximized other places – like your family, various leadership challenges, or even spots of rest for you.

In order to study less, preachers must come to grips with the truth that a sermon they see as possessing 100% effectiveness with 25 hours of preparation is not really that much different to their listeners than a message at 90% effectiveness with 15 hours of preparation. Trust me, the only people who are bothered by that missing 10% are the preachers. Congregations won't notice the difference at all. If by some miracle they can, you can add hours as needed, but I'd bet most congregations wouldn't even blink at hearing a message that took 15 hours to prepare versus one that took 25. If that's true of the congregation, why wouldn't you do your church, family, and your health a favor by studying less? Some questions to consider:

- *What is your sermon's saturation point?*
- *How many hours does it really take until you find your message at the incremental phase?*
- *What areas of your life need to gain monumental hours from your incremental hours in sermon prep?*

Answering those honestly and courageously can be the difference between surviving in ministry and thriving in it. With those extra hours reallocated to other critical endeavors week-in and week-out, you'll be more equipped on Sunday to put your skis over the edge and take your congregation down the mountain. Honestly, do you need to study less?

BEWARE OF THE SEDUCTION OF STUDY

I hope my words don't give the impression that pastors should be light on sermon preparation. Personally, studying for my sermons is one of my favorite ministry tasks. One of the chief reasons is because it affords me the opportunity to study God's Word in-depth for a concentrated season with tools like commentaries, lexicons, and other hermeneutical aids. In fact, I frequently find myself joyously blown away by some new insight or truth about the biblical text I hadn't seen before. Those moments give me such excitement.

And yet it is in those very moments when my sermon hangs in the balance for Sunday. Some might wonder why, because they've been instructed that the times a pastor feels especially impassioned or moved by certain insights into the Scriptures in his study are the ones that will make his message all the better. The problem is that this isn't necessarily true.

Indeed, I'll go so far as to say that what blows you away in the study may bore people to death in the sanctuary. So many preachers take congregants on a specific turn in their journey down the mountain in Sunday's sermon, convinced the point's insight and erudition will leave everyone in awe. Yet mere moments into the turn, they're shocked to see glassed-over eyes and even a head or two drooping in slumber. Can you feel yourself tumbling down the run? The best you can hope for at this point is that you didn't build everything else in your message around this "amazing" insight.[36] If you did, I'm sorry. Welcome to the K-12.

While sermon study for most preachers is a time of joyous work, there is also a seduction within it. The temptation is to use on Sunday anything and everything which deeply grabs us about the text we're preaching. But this is where we should ask a question: *Will my congregants be as excited as I am about certain things I discovered in my study?* You know which things I'm referring to – the ones which aren't germane to the sermon's fall line, but are so

---

[36] By 'amazing' I mean it amazingly tunes people out from your message.

theologically or exegetically juicy that you can't bear to part with them come Sunday.

Understand that this will hamstring your messages more than you think. It's the extra turn down the mountain that ruins the run for everyone except the guy leading it. If we constantly find ourselves in this pattern on Sundays, a rebuke may even be in order. Because when preaching becomes more about you than those to whom you preach, it's a homiletical form of selfishness. As discussed in an earlier chapter, it's more about our felt need to say it than the congregants' real need not to hear it. However, from my perspective, this struggle isn't usually rooted in selfishness but in an inability to discern what's cool to us from what's helpful for others.

If we more closely examine our feelings during sermon study, what we interpret as inspiring might simply be us "geeking out" because we've stumbled over something which produces in us a pathos that only a few of the most theologically literate would share. That's why the question to ask is not, "Is this compelling to me?" but, "Will this be compelling to them?"[37] If what you are learning only causes you to lean forward in the study without your congregants doing the same in the pew, it's probably not worth using on Sunday. Put it in the non-compelling category or what I call the "Do Not Use" pile. Frankly, my "Do Not Use" pile and my "What's Incredibly Interesting to Yancey" pile often are the same thing.

Does that mean I preach things that aren't interesting to me? Not at all! I just try to make sure it will also be interesting to those listening. You might be asking, "But why, Yancey, would God move me so deeply if he didn't want me to use it Sunday?" Could it be that God wants to use those moments to impact the character of the preacher rather than the content of his preaching? Is it possible that what moved you in the study this week is what God will use to

---

[37] I recognize sometimes this isn't due to a content issue but a delivery issue. In other words, the reason people don't lean in is simply due to poor preaching.

impact how you say something else? Hopefully the what of your sermon has unity, cohesion, and laser-like focus on a main idea. Whatever exegetical or theological insights that don't carry listeners with pace down the fall line of the main idea – no matter how cool you believe those insights to be – need to stay with you in the study and not proceed to the pulpit. If you want to be ready to drop your skis over the edge on Sunday, learn how to harness the beauty of study while fleeing its temptation at the same time.

CONCLUSION

Leverage your week in the best possible way, so that when you finally stand atop the mountain of your message, peering over the tips of your skis, you'll know all that is left is to take the plunge. Take that plunge with the confidence that instead of falling down, hitting a tree, or leaving your followers scattered throughout the run, you will guide your listeners on a journey through God's Word that will move them in a way that grows their hearts in the gospel and brings joy to the one who preaches.

Are you ready to take the plunge?

FIND YOUR VOICE

8
FIND YOUR VOICE

"Be yourself. Everyone else is already taken."

– OSCAR WILDE

My wife, Jennefer, is a wonderful skier. Some of our favorite memories are framed around skiing together. She would even say that it was at a Colorado ski resort where we began to fall in love.

We spent the day, just the two of us, hitting run after run. And although we don't get to go as often as we would like anymore, we have both loved skiing ever since. One of the things I like about skiing with Jennefer is that her style of attacking a slope is completely different from mine. She playfully says that I'm concerned about skiing "pretty." It's important for me to use good form – things like planting my poles correctly, shifting my weight on the outside ski, and keeping my upper body pointed downhill. I also like to take my time carving up the run. I feel like this allows me to maximize the skiing experience.

But Jennefer is a different story. Her style is simple: point the ski tips downhill and go as fast as you responsibly can. We'll do a run together, and no sooner than I reach my first or second turn, she'll dart past me with a huge smile under her goggles. I love it. Each of us ski our own way. It's the way that feels best to us. Each style fits our personalities. There is no question Jen could ski "pretty" if she liked, and I could turn on the afterburners if I wanted, but neither of us would be skiing the way that fits us. Doing so might detract from the experience. We each have our own way of getting down the mountain.

The same holds true for preaching. Each of us, based on our God-given personalities, has a unique way to get down the mountain of our messages. Some love to preach using their hands, while others stay relatively still. Some raise their voices in dramatic fashion, while others keep a more conversational tone. The list of differences seems unending. The big question is not if you are different in the pulpit, but how are you different? What makes you unique? What's your way of getting down the mountain? In order to preach in a way that moves people, pastors must not only address the *how* of preaching, but the *who* as well. The common phrase used to refer to a preacher's embracing his unique way of getting down the mountain is to "find one's voice."

Lawrence E. Aker III shares the story of a colleague offering him congratulations following his Sunday message, to which Aker replied, "Thanks, but for what?" The man answered, "I think you've finally found your own voice." Aker interpreted the gentleman's statement to mean that he had finally "found the freedom, power, and authority to let the Holy Spirit use [him]...I finally felt comfortable in my own skin as a preacher. I had learned so much from other preachers—especially my predecessors—but now I wasn't just mimicking someone else."[38]

What a wonderful place for a preacher to be. Skiing free indeed! I'm sure there are many pastors who, early in their preaching tenures, knew exactly who they were in the pulpit. Using Aker's terminology, they felt at ease with themselves, comfortable in their own skin, and preached within their personalities from day one. They weren't prone to copying or mimicking other pastors they admired. They were good with themselves as themselves. In short,

---

[38] http://www.preachingtoday.com/skills/2013/january/finding-your-own-preaching-voice.html

they had found their voice.

Alas, I was not one of those preachers. Like Aker, I can personally vouch that my initial foray into the world of preaching was simultaneously a quest to find my own voice in the pulpit. It took years of preaching sermons before I finally arrived at a place where I felt like the guy in the pulpit was me. Better yet, I was actually happy it was me. I had finally rid myself of feeling the need to be someone else in the preaching event. But make no mistake, it did take time.

I believe the majority of preachers, especially those early in their ministries, have to tread a rather lengthy path to find their voice. Popular author and pastor Kevin DeYoung gives us some perspective on his travel down this road: "Since 2002, the year I was ordained, I estimate that I've preached almost 500 times. It took about 450 sermons to find my voice."[39]

That is about a decade's worth of preaching, or a lot of runs down the mountain, to say the least! Of course there are exceptions, but they only prove the rule that, for most of us, getting comfortable in our own skin as preachers is going to take some time. But no matter how long it takes, finding your voice is critical for preaching that moves people. Failing to do so prevents you from maximizing your contribution as the unique preacher God designed you to be.

FRANKENSERMONS

You don't necessarily have to be a rookie preacher to struggle with this issue. There are older, seasoned pastors who have yet to find their voice because they still parrot someone else's preaching style. They point their tips when they should be carving slowly down the mountain, or vice versa. Sometimes what they produce in the pulpit is an admixture of multiple preachers who they admire but aren't anything like. This produces Sunday sermons that devolve into a Frankensteinian experiment where messages are unnaturally fused

---

[39]http://www.christianitytoday.com/le/2010/winter/findingyourownvoice.html

together with elements alien to the preacher's personality. Maybe it's an intensely emotional plea from someone with a relatively small emotional bandwidth, or a technical exposition from someone who isn't adept at original languages or academic terminology, or relating a humorous story from someone who has no sense of comedic timing. It doesn't matter. The results of each ill-fitting activity produce a monstrous sermon experience for listeners. The preacher obscures himself behind his freakish creation of a sermon that's ineffective, if not downright awkward, for the congregation. It's moving for all the wrong reasons. Stay away from Frankensermons!

While this kind of preaching doesn't always equate to a science experiment gone awry, it still takes a toll on both preacher and congregants. Want to burn out as a preacher? Preach outside your personality. It's taxing, exhausting, and joyless. If you experience any of those feelings Sunday after Sunday, it could very well be that you're trying to don someone else's persona when you preach.

This is why preaching that moves people involves more than focusing one's attention on just the message. It must also address the messenger as well. Pastors should commit to not only prepare messages with proper emotional flow, but also to preach them with their unique, God-given personalities. Preaching that moves people demands that every preacher find his voice.

The next section of this book will give practical ways preachers can make sure that the voice they preach with is their own, and in doing so, preach in a way that moves people. The key is to know, embrace, and leverage your style of going down the mountain. And while it might take some time, don't' fear! The following chapters in this section are dedicated to expediting that process by offering practical steps to help ensure that when you step into the pulpit, you bring one of the most critical components of preaching that moves people: *you*.

9
IDENTIFY YOUR
PREACHING PERSONALITY

*"Preaching is the bringing
of truth through personality."*
– PHILLIPS BROOKS

Whitle skiers may come in a myriad of varieties, preachers can be grouped into four personality types by my count. Most have a primary and secondary style. These different categories aren't a commentary on the quality of sermon delivery or content, only the manner in which the message is preached. Each style has wonderful examples of preaching within it (I'll supply a representative or two). The aim is to identify which of the four personalities best represents you, in order that you would embrace its strengths and leverage them in the preaching event. Acknowledging that there are exceptions with any generalization, here are the four preaching personality styles.

#1: The Professor
Strength: *Insightful with information.*

The Professor makes complex ideas understandable for congregants. He easily connects the dots of different truths most preachers would miss. Professors get excited at new concepts or subtle doctrinal discoveries, and want their listeners to understand why those finds are so important. This preaching personality tends to dedicate a lot of time in messages to abstract or theological concepts. What makes them different from other preaching personalities is their ease and elegance in making those rather complex concepts appealing to their listeners. Listeners always feel like they learn something new about the subject at hand. Sermons given by Professors are well-constructed, logical in flow, and packed with information. They also can have more sub-points than an IRS form.

Emotional bandwidth: Smallest emotional range of the four personalities. Messages can tend to feel lecture-oriented.

Example: Tim Keller, D.A. Carson

#2: The Author
Strength: *Insightful with observation.*

The Author cannot preach without telling a story for his congregants that demonstrates how an idea fleshes itself out in real-time. Authors have an incredible knack for describing life in a way listeners can both identify and inhabit. They can open up the listener's daily life in a sensory fashion, using their superior descriptive powers in storytelling. Authors can be obsessed with word-crafting. They feel compelled to deliver their content the "right way." Thus, Authors tend to be married to their sermon notes (generally, in manuscript form). They don't desire to speak off the cuff because that would derail them from their air-tight manuscript. I often joke that one could take an Author's sermon notes, three-hole punch them, and simply send it off to a publisher without missing a beat. This may also be the reason why I see Authors keep their head down when preaching more than other personality types.

Emotional bandwidth: Varied.

Example: John Ortberg, Max Lucado

#3: The Life Coach
Strength: *Insightful with application.*

The Life Coach possesses the uncanny ability to exegete his congregants' daily life with incredible precision. The sermon's "rubber meets the road" sections cause listeners to wonder if the preacher has been reading their mail. If, as John Stott once said, the sermon is a journey between the world of the Bible and the world of the listener[40], the Life Coach has a masterful grasp of the latter, especially when it comes to sermon application. This is the primary thrust of a Life Coach's message. Listeners come away thinking about the amount of wisdom they've received, because the Life Coach is so adept at giving insightful, helpful next steps. The preaching style of this personality is mostly informal and conversational.

Emotional bandwidth: Varied. While a message may be peppered with more intense emotional elements, I find most Life Coaches to be fairly relaxed in overall delivery.

Examples: Andy Stanley, Rick Warren

---

[40] John Stott, *Between Two Worlds: The Challenge of Preaching Today* (Eerdmans, 1994)

#4: The Prophet
Strength: *Insightful with conviction.*

The Prophet sees the disconnect between what is and what should be. Prophets tend to be naturally expressive teachers who not only want you to hear what they're saying, but to feel what they're saying. They run to conflict and love to engage the emotional tension in their listeners. They are also generally more physically demonstrative. In contrast to Professors, Prophets say more with less material because they tend to be more spontaneous or off-the-cuff speakers. Unlike Authors, Prophets feel hampered by reading their notes for any extended period of time. It eats at them to keep their head down in their notes instead of heads up with their listeners. Prophets can go on tangents, lose themselves in the message, and regard fixed sermon lengths as a nice idea...for someone else.

Emotional bandwidth: Largest emotional range. They can cry, shout, laugh all within a three-minute period, and yet it makes emotional sense to their listeners.

Examples: John Piper, Matt Chandler

Prophet – professor?

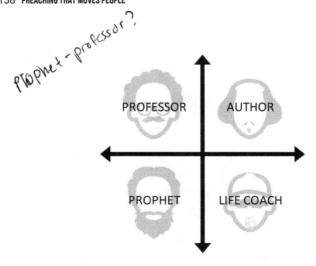

PROFESSOR   AUTHOR

PROPHET   LIFE COACH

Which of these personalities do you resemble? What is your primary and secondary style? Do you see elements of other preaching personalities that aren't primary or secondary? Once again, generalizations necessitate exceptions. However, the point of knowing your style is not to typecast but encourage you to find your voice in the pulpit. If you are an Author trying to preach like a Prophet, it's going to drain you. If you are a Professor trying to act like a Life Coach, you are creating frustration for yourself. Remember, if you want to preach to move others, you must first be you! It's much more beneficial for your congregants to have a strong you in the pulpit than a poor version of someone else. Knowing your personality is a big step in finding your voice because once you identify your God-given wiring, you can begin leveraging the strengths within it.

EMBRACE YOUR STRENGTHS

Stylistically, I'm a *Prophet*. I express emotional highs and lows with relative ease. Humor also comes naturally for me. However, early in my preaching ministry there was a season where I began to resent my wiring for humor. I would routinely hear people compliment my preaching by singling out a humorous story or idea I shared and never mention anything about the point of the sermon. Although these individuals weren't saying that my messages didn't have substance, I took it as such. Although I would smile and thank them for the compliment, internally, it would eat me up. I would silently (and somewhat defiantly) declare to myself, "I'm a preacher, not a comedian!" Consequently, I began to intentionally remove humor from my messages. I would prove to everyone that I didn't need that specific part of me to be an effective preacher!

However, as I matured in ministry and developed a confidence in the content of my sermons, I realized that completely removing humor from my preaching wasn't leveraging all of my God-given personality. While I readily acknowledge that humor can be used in a detrimental way that trivializes preaching, I had chosen to cut it entirely from my messages. I was offering both to God and my congregation a lesser version of myself in the pulpit. By not properly utilizing humor within my preaching, I was poorly stewarding the personality God gave me. In order to be the preacher I needed to be, I had to embrace all of my personality, not just some of it. The same holds true for you.

Discovering your personality is important in finding your voice, because it encourages you to not only know your strengths but harness them in the pulpit. Imagine preaching each Sunday knowing that you're bringing to bear everything God wired you to be. Each preaching personality has wonderful strengths that should be leveraged in the pulpit. You have important traits that can and should be rightfully used when you preach. So, what are they? Discuss the four preaching personality types with those who know you. Ask which ones (primary and secondary) they see in you. Once you've done that, let them share with you what they believe your strengths are when you open God's Word to preach. Do you excel at storytelling? Are you funny? Do you give wonderful insights? Are you strong in message application?

Community reflection is incredibly helpful because we tend to see ourselves as we want to see ourselves. We self-project. For example, you may think that you are funny, insightful, or strong in giving application when, in reality, few others see those same traits. The problem is they feel no pressing need to tell you what they see in you – that takes a boldness which often comes only by invitation. So, invite them! Every preaching personality has areas in which they excel that can be leveraged in the preaching event, but you must own and embrace the personality (and its accompanying strengths) that you actually possess. Identifying this will allow you to better steward your development as a preacher. Now you can spend time in the pulpit sharpening those areas and increasing your preaching prowess, instead of wasting years by focusing on things in which you don't naturally excel. It's one more reason why discovering your preaching personality and the strengths it brings is such a big step in finding your voice.

RETHINK YOUR PRESENCE

Professor and author James K.A. Smith reminds us that followers of Jesus, as human beings, aren't just intellectual creatures but embodied ones as well.[41] We aren't merely "thinking-thingisms," who need to consider only the mental aspects of our composition, but the physical or corporal importance of our makeup as well. When comedians try to impersonate a movie star, pro athlete, or president, they don't only change their voice but mannerisms too. They try to "embody" those they parody because the essence of someone's personality isn't merely verbal but physical as well. Comedians must include it all to truly im-*person*-ate someone. Our personalities give animation to our bodies. This is no less true for the pulpit.

I would encourage pastors to rethink their presence in front of the congregation. "Real" preaching doesn't demand someone stoically stand behind a pulpit, hands affixed to each side. Nor does it mean authentic preaching must be done by pacing to and fro sans podium. I think it's too easy for some to be rather legalistic about

---

[41] James K.A. Smith, *You Are What You Love: The Spiritual Power of Habit*, 6, 46.

the preacher's physical setup. I remember when it was fashionable to critique pastors who preached sitting atop a stool. It was as if being seated made the sermon less a sermon, and Christ gave you a lower grade on the evaluation sheet. But didn't Jesus, according to rabbinical tradition, sit down to teach? What do you do with passages like John 8:2, "Early in the morning he came again to the temple. All the people came to him, and he *sat down* and taught them."?[42] What a scandal! Could it be those who preach perched upon stools are actually more biblically Christ-like in their physical expressions than those who stand behind pulpits?

All joking aside, I would argue that in whatever fashion our personalities best animate our physical bodies as we preach, that should frame how we carry ourselves before the congregation.

What preaching posture matches you? Do you feel best standing behind a pulpit? If you speak with your hands, it might be better to have a podium or music stand at your side, freeing you to gesticulate in more natural ways. If you speak with a more conversational than declarative tone, a table or stool might be to your liking. Whatever you fancy, I hope the point is clear: pick a posture that fits your personality. I'm amazed to hear preachers share how much more effectively and joyfully they preach after simply changing the physical setup for their preaching.

While rethinking your presence won't write your sermons for you, it can free you up to preach those sermons as the "you" God made you to be. It's also just one more step in leveraging your God-given personality and helping find your voice in preaching.

---

[42] See also Mt. 5:1, Lk. 5:3, Mt. 13:2

10

INFLUENCES OR IDOLS

"I want to be a clone."

– STEVE TAYLOR

I began skiing in junior high on a church trip to Santa Fe, New Mexico. Most of my close friends had been skiing since grade school, so on the first day at the mountain I headed to ski-school by myself. It lasted only half a day before I snuck away with my friends. It wasn't that I didn't need to be trained, but rather I had more than enough people offer to do the teaching as we skied together. They were patient and kind, and I had a blast. By the end of the day, I was skiing runs that gave me the feeling that I was almost one of them. I couldn't ski all the runs they chose, but I could do some. I also noticed that I not only wanted to just ski *with* them, but I wanted to ski *like* them. I wanted to jump moguls like this friend, carve through turns like that friend, or spray snow with a "hockey stop" like this other friend. My friends weren't just my teachers. They were my influencers. I needed to have some kind of model for skiing, so I started with those I already admired.

Preachers also have influences, fellow pulpiteers they admire – some from afar, some within the same church – but every pastor has them. All of us have been influenced in some way or another in our preaching. As the old adage says, "Things are more caught than taught." This is true in both skiing and preaching. It's natural to find young pastors often starting their preaching ministries by mimicking those they admire. However, imitation is like putting training wheels on a bicycle: it's extremely helpful for beginners, but eventually maturity demands that we journey on our own. If not, the practice of preaching, like bicycling with assistance once you have learned to ride, becomes a restrictive experience. It turns into something less than what it is meant to be.

The question is not will you be influenced by other preachers, but which preachers have already influenced you? Are there preachers currently influencing your preaching and in what ways? Which of all these influences has helped you move closer to finding your voice or, possibly, pushed you away from it? Are you getting down the mountain in a forced fashion, instead of a more natural way? Furthermore, how do you know if those influences have now become idols?

While influences help refine our preaching voice, idols prevent us from ever finding it. They retard our growth as sermonizers and hamper us from preaching in a way that moves people. It's a sure way to consistently create Frankensermons that bear little resemblance to the real thing.

Finding your voice demands examining your preaching influences, and discerning whether you have influences or idols. The reality for many is that they have both. Here are some practical steps that may allow you to affirm the former while minimizing the latter, all in hopes of making sure that the voice you use in the pulpit is yours.

TRACE YOUR INFLUENCES

Hebrews 13:7 reads: "Remember your leaders, those who spoke to you the word of God. Consider the outcome of their way of life, and imitate their faith." While this instruction is given to the entire congregation of believers, I've seen how it intersects my preaching life. Everyone is influenced by those they admire, and preachers are no different, especially young ones.

I can almost categorize my development as a sermonizer by referencing certain pulpiteers who, at different stages in my life, impacted me as I sat under their preaching (via tapes[43], podcasts, live, etc.). My intention in listening to them was to better learn the Bible, yet I found my preaching being influenced by theirs. Here's the diagram of my line of influences:

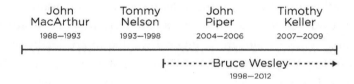

Listening to each of these individuals had profound effects on my preaching. During my college years, the Lord used John MacArthur to give me an insatiable love for God's Word and a growing passion for verse-by-verse expositional preaching. Over my seminary career, God used the pulpit ministry of Denton Bible Church's Tommy Nelson to emphasize that sermons must be more than a running commentary on a Bible passage but fleshed out in the lives of the listener via story and illustration. In the initial years after seminary and early tenure at my current church, God used the sermons of John Piper to remind me that passion behind the pulpit is not peripheral, but essential, to preaching.

In more recent times, I've seen God's grace to me via the gospel-centric pulpit ministry of Tim Keller. His words both in preaching, and about preaching, have reaffirmed my commitment to making sure Christ is the center of my messages. Each week, after finishing my sermon notes, I ask myself this question: "Why did Jesus have to die for this message?" If I don't know the answer, my work is not done.

---

[43] A cassette tape (Compact Cassette) is a recording format of a bygone era, often played on ancient technologies like a Walkman or boom box.

Last, but not least, is Bruce Wesley, the pastor with whom I share the pulpit week-in and week-out. God has used Bruce to teach me more about preaching than I can ever itemize. At the writing of this chapter, a few things stand out: the power of wordsmithing, the utility of manuscripting, and the practice of anticipating the listener's objections are aspects of Bruce's preaching which have impacted my own.

I confess, early in my ministry these men were more likely idols than influences. I didn't want to learn from them. I wanted to be them. I wanted to be as technical as MacArthur, as illustrative as Nelson, and as passionate at Piper. I wanted to artificially import their strengths into my preaching. Unfortunately, it made for a poor composition in the pulpit. My voice was constantly being lost, and Frankensermons abounded as I abdicated my true personality for false ones.

There is a great difference between learning from someone's preaching and cheaply copying it. Models will help you in the pulpit, while idols will crush you there. Tracing your line of influences will provide more objectivity in analyzing what is yours in the pulpit and what you've forcibly imported from someone else. It refines the search for our voice by discerning our preaching influences and allowing them to be critically analyzed as it intersects our own preaching profile.

PAUSE YOUR PODCASTS

As my line of influence reveals, I spent my college years listening to tons of cassettes from the preaching ministry of John MacArthur. This was in addition to faithfully hearing his weekly radio program *Grace to You*, as well as *The Alternative* with Tony Evans.[44] But I wasn't finished. Toward the end of my college career, I added other preachers like Tommy Nelson to my preacher's playlist.

Though I listened to them in order to grow in God's Word, I also

---

[44] I affectionately referred to these back-to-back 30-minute programs as "The Hour of Power."

subconsciously looked to them as models for preaching. Many (if not most) preachers, especially those who are trying to find their voice in the pulpit, gain inspiration from listening to pulpiteers they admire. The internet today, with its world of podcasts, downloads, and online messages, gives greater access to the preaching ministry of others than ever before. If you want to hear from a specific preacher, regardless of the size of his church, chances are you can dial up his sermons in less than five minutes.

Yet I would humbly suggest that those who've yet to find their voice in the pulpit consider pausing their podcasts for a season. It's too great a temptation for some young sermonizers to listen regularly to preachers they admire, because they don't yet have enough wherewithal internally to know where the influence of their heroes should stop. If one isn't careful, healthy admiration in front of the computer can turn into unhealthy imitation behind the pulpit.

Don't misunderstand – this doesn't mean you shouldn't learn from other preachers. Just be careful that you are learning from other preachers to become a better you, not a poorer version of them. Pastor and author Joshua Harris, reflecting on his own playlist preachers, humorously noted, "In my teen years, I idolized Billy Graham and Ravi Zacharias. I listened to so many Zacharias sermons I actually started speaking with a slight Indian accent, which must have baffled my audiences."[45] While I think that's hilarious, it's also a good reminder that we may not realize how powerful a sway preaching podcasts have over us. They can tempt us to preach in ways that are outside our personality – far from our natural bandwidth or real voice. It's the sermonic equivalent of asking Willie Nelson to sing Heavy Metal. Nobody benefits from that.

Consider pausing your podcasts for a season in order to better find who you are in the pulpit, rather than who you would like to be. Who knows? It may free you up to discover other strengths in yourself than those you hear in others. It will also move you closer

---

[45] http://www.christianitytoday.com/le/2010/winter/findingyourownvoice.html

to finding your voice.

KNOW YOUR ROLE

Finding your voice also demands that you, the preacher, realize it's not your personality strengths, oral articulation, or ministry skill-set that changes people. As noted earlier in this book, transformation is uniquely the role of the Holy Spirit. The preacher's job is to allow God's Spirit to work through him as he displays how Christ is the sum and substance of the Scriptures. In 1 Corinthians 3:7, the Apostle Paul reminded a congregation who had been debating which pulpiteer was their favorite that "neither he who plants nor he who waters is anything, but only God who gives the growth." Each of the men who alighted the Corinthian pulpit, regardless of their personal preaching strength or weakness, were simply "God's fellow workers." (1 Cor. 3:9) All of these individuals were essential instruments of God's grace, but not agents. The agency through which the Corinthians were transformed is a role reserved only for the sovereign God.

In Acts 2:46-47, we witness the regular practices of the early church:

> And day by day, attending the temple together and breaking bread in their homes, they received their food with glad and generous hearts, praising God and having favor with all the people. And the Lord added to their number day by day those who were being saved.

Who is doing the preaching? Who is leading these followers of Jesus to exhibit the habits and virtues of the kingdom observed in this passage? Who is expositing the Scripture in such a way that Christ is seen, adored, and received? While we can be sure it is the collective work of apostolic ministry, the text singles out no specific human individual. On the contrary, the spotlight of who is behind the catalytic growth of the church falls squarely upon God. It is through his sovereign power that the church had "added to their number day by day those who were being saved." The roles in Christ's church are clear: our job is to share; God's job is to save.

Too often young pastors see the "success" of other preachers (often in the form of large, growing churches and, to a lesser extent, the fool's gold of book deals, conference invites, or an extensive social media following) and wonder if they can assimilate enough of the characteristics of their preaching that they would begin to achieve similar results. But succumbing to this temptation only further obfuscates the search for one's voice. The carrot of church growth success dangles from the end of a stick held by pastors whose preaching styles may be nothing like your own. The novice (and not so novice) preacher fails to realize that what works for others may hurt him because the attributes of those he admires in preaching are so counter to his unique, God-designed voice.

Frankly, at the risk of sounding cynical, it could be that some pastors' success may have more to do with creating a dog-and-pony show where, among other unhelpful but overly-pragmatic church activities, the preaching is nothing more than a man-centered pep talk that is light on the Scriptures and even lighter on the gospel. Why did they adopt this biblically shallow approach to sermonizing? Simply put, it attracts a crowd. However, a crowd does not a congregation make.

There are far too many undiscerning pastors who, dismayed by lack of attendance each Sunday, are tempted to emulate the kind of preaching which is crowd-building but not congregation-growing. They want the kind of "success" they see in these high-profile preachers. Yet, what they fail to understand is that this type of crowd-building preaching, ironically, subverts the roles pastors are given. Whenever we preach in a fashion that manipulates for numbers, like preaching the Bible as a self-help manual, or as one more guide to a better suburban life, it belies what we really believe about what God does in the preaching event. It's as if our role as human instrument isn't big enough. We want to add to the numbers ourselves instead of trusting God to fulfill his role in the agency of transformation.

But trusting God, in his sovereign goodness, as the one who brings people to salvation and increases the sanctification of his saints via the preaching of the Word should free us up to be us. If the Lord's role is to save and our role to share, then any genuine, spiritual success we see from the pulpit ultimately is the work of God in us and around us. It has nothing to do with our personalities. John Piper wrote:

> You can mark it down that if you are a preacher God will hide from you much of the fruit he causes in your ministry. You will see enough to be assured of his blessing, but not so much as to think you could live without it. For God aims to exalt himself, not the preacher.[46]

One of the surest ways to delay discovering your voice in the pulpit is to choose a crowd over a congregation. To look for preaching techniques and tricks that drive up numbers is forgetting our true role as a preacher. It's to place our trust in the chariots and horses of human ingenuity and achievement instead of trusting God to accomplish his purposes (Ps. 20:7). Knowing our role as preachers, and the rightful place our personalities have within the preaching event, liberates us from the need to adopt unbiblical preaching strategies while also keeping our influences from becoming idols.

KEEP INFLUENCES, NOT IDOLS

Having my friends as models during my initial foray into skiing definitely gave me an advantage. I mimicked what they did on the slopes, and for the first couple of years it paid off. But I cannot imagine flying down a run still tethered to my friends' examples. I had to grow as a skier over time. I needed to develop my own style

---

[46] John Piper, *The Supremacy of God in Preaching* (Grand Rapids: Baker, 2004), 19.

– my own "voice" on the slopes. No longer did I want to ski deep powder like this friend, or navigate moguls like that friend. I needed to develop my own way of doing things. Doing so has enabled me not only to ski in a way that is effective but also brings me great joy. May the same hold true for us as preachers. Keep your influences as influences, not idols, so you might get down the mountain of a Sunday message with great effectiveness and joy!

11

MOVING FORWARD

"I fear preaching in such a way that
when people hear about God, they'll want only to yawn."
— HADDON ROBINSON

As much as I learned from watching my friends on the slopes, at some point I actually had to ski. I knew the more I skied, the more I would be able to get down the mountain in ways I loved. It would be a lot of trial and error, but there were no shortcuts. How could friends help me further develop if I didn't make myself hit the same runs they did? I had to keep skiing to find out who I would be as a skier. In the same way, you have to preach if you want to find out who you are as a preacher.

Beyond identifying someone's preaching personality and the influences that have shaped a person's voice in preaching, the final area to address in finding one's voice is the individual's actual preaching. You must hit the slopes of Sunday mornings to develop into who God called you to be. How can preachers use their preaching to move closer to their real voice in the pulpit and, consequently, better preach in a way that moves people? Here are some specific steps to take within your preaching ministry so that you might more quickly find your voice as you get down the mountain of your messages.

GET YOUR RUNS

There may be no better advice for discovering your voice in the pulpit than to simply keep preaching. The more you preach, the more you'll get a feel for who you are as a preacher. Thus, a sure road to finding your voice is to get your reps. While I don't think there is a magic number of sermons you must preach to find your voice, I do believe there is a number of messages given, and that number is probably not a small one. Keep hitting those runs as often as you can!

That shouldn't be too discouraging if you are a lead or senior pastor whose role entails regularly preaching; it's only a matter of time before you eventually feel comfortable with being you in the pulpit. At least that's the hope. But what if you aren't one of the primary sermonizers at your church? I would suggest, especially for my friends who are just beginning to work on their preaching gift, that you look for as many places as possible to get in as many runs as possible. In my early 20's, I preached in retirement homes, Fellowship of Christian Athletes gatherings, student ministry retreats, and even at churches that were in-between pastors. My goal was simply to get as many runs as possible, as early as possible. I knew I had a long way to go in developing my preaching gift and discovering who God made me to be in the pulpit. If there was a specific number of sermons that I needed to preach to find my voice, the sooner I got there the better. So, to all my beloved young guns: get in your runs. The more times you experience taking others down the mountain of a message, the better you will become at it. Preach wherever you can, and whenever you can, to both develop your gift and better find your voice.

FIND YOUR FEEDBACK

Evaluation isn't a bad word at my church. We do it often. It helps us avoid repeating the same mistakes and raises the level of excellence in future ministry endeavors. One of the areas we evaluate with regularity is preaching. For example, after the first of three Sunday services I meet with a handful of our elders to hear from them about the good, bad, and ugly in my sermon. Don't worry, it's not a firing squad, but brothers who are familiar with the demands and designs of preaching. They know my personality and how it should express itself in the pulpit. They help me make sure I'm using my voice.

Having that weekly evaluation is a good and healthy thing for our church's pulpit ministry. When it's my turn to evaluate others, I usually go in this order:

- *Tell me what you liked about the message.*
- *What do you wish you could have done differently?*[47]
- *Here is what I liked about your message.*
- *Here are some things to consider for the next time you preach this message.*

I like repeating this process because it lets those under evaluation know what to expect from me. I'm not surprising them or springing something new on them. On the contrary, it allows them to get the first shot at examining their message. I want them to tell me how they felt getting down the mountain before I share my observations. I have given evaluations of preaching and received the same, and I can definitely affirm that I wouldn't be half the preacher I am today without this kind of feedback.

When we do Sunday morning evaluations, we make sure the preacher can actually use that information to help with the next service. If the feedback deals with something bigger or more complex than what could be resolved in the next preaching event, we call that a "Monday Conversation." I don't want to burden the preacher's thoughts with something that really needs more time to address than the 30-minute interval before the next service. The evaluation we give is focused purely on what can directly help the

---

[47] Because evaluation is always a personal thing, I like to let the *preacher-under-evaluation* first identify what he didn't like about his sermon. That way, if he points to something I also noticed, I don't have to bring it up. Doing so helps alleviate unnecessary discouragement that the one being evaluated might feel.

preacher before the next service.

Good feedback also demands what we call giving "the last 10%." This refers to that little piece of evaluation that people hold back because they don't want to hurt someone's feelings. However, more times than not, if a person is going to grow as a preacher, it's that very last piece of evaluation they most need to hear. This doesn't give us license to share the last 10% however we like. We give it as we would want to receive it – with grace, kindness, and thoughtfulness. Still, if we are trying to develop preachers who are more adept at leading congregations down the mountain of our messages, that means giving the last 10%.

Let me encourage you to form a team of people who not only know what preaching is about but what you are about. Find those familiar with your unique emotional bandwidth who know you *as you*. These are folk who know you well enough to identify moments where you've preached outside of yourself. Make sure that these individuals would be able to kindly give you the last 10%. It's not for everyone. For example, if our spouses are wired to be encouragers who will tell us we've done well no matter what, then don't put them on the evaluative team. They are already playing roles we also need. Make it your mission to find others who, by their consistent and caring feedback, can help you grow in getting down the mountain.

EVALUATION AND BANDWIDTH

Before leaving the topic of feedback, let's return to the practice of charting your bandwidth. So far, we have talked about how preachers do this for their message development; however, let me encourage you to orient your feedback team in this practice as well. If you do, they can employ the idea of the chart in the evaluative process. Let me explain.

As I note earlier, preachers have within the bandwidth of their personalities a natural zone that best contains their emotional highs and lows. Going beyond this zone creates a "bull factor" to preaching. In my home state of Texas, the word "bull" is shorthand for something that's trying to pass itself off as real but isn't. When you preach in a way foreign to your personality, listeners feel someone other than you is preaching. This is where it would benefit a pastor to have those who can lovingly point out when he has entered into the bull factor zone.

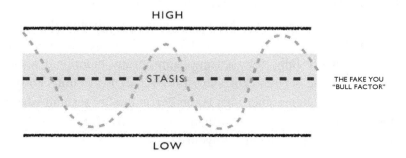

I saw this evidenced in a staff member who was tasked to preach on a Sunday at one of our campuses. In the first of two services, I noticed his sermon was very well-prepared. However, while his content was water-tight, the delivery was misfiring. My friend spoke very softly, even quietly to the point you had to perk up your ears to hear what he was saying. It felt slow and almost syrupy. That's not necessarily bad, but it was nothing like who he is personality-wise. Frankly, the delivery came across as preachy in a manufactured way. It was the emotional equivalent of the sermonizers of yesteryear who took upon themselves some kind of special "preaching voice" which is nothing like their real voice.

Some of you know what I'm talking about. It's the well-meaning pastor who naturally has a high-pitched register but magically produces a deep bass intonation while pronouncing words. The dichotomy between what is seen out of the pulpit with what is seen in it feels contrived in today's culture. It's as if preaching brings with it a Dr. Jekyll and Mr. Hyde transformation. In short, if the person you see in the pulpit isn't the same person out of it, that's when a preacher has moved into the bull factor zone.

And for my staff friend, his sermon's bull factor was high. After the service concluded, the campus pastor and I found our friend and told him in tandem, "We appreciate the effort you're giving, but that's not you out there. You never talk that softly or posture yourself that way. Just relax. Trust in who you are. Just be you." He received our counsel, and the second service went tremendously better. He simply preached within his natural bandwidth.

Preachers can also live too thinly inside their bandwidth. This is what I call the "bored factor." It's named as such because the preacher never fully demonstrates appropriate emotional levels throughout the sermon but stays rather flat. Everything hovers around stasis. Remember, this is the Ferris Bueller sermon where the preacher gives the emotional equivalent of the tone-deaf staccato: "Anyone? Anyone? Anyone?"

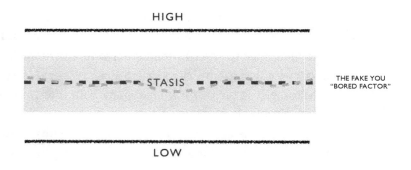

I was listening to a sermon given by another one of our gifted young staffers we want to develop in preaching for the future. This particular "gun" is a hyper-talented seminary grad, full of incredible potential as both a leader and a preacher. When afforded a Sunday morning to preach before our congregation, his sermon moved with verve, animation, and presence. His message was incredibly well-constructed and surely would have scored well in homiletics class (this individual had actually won an award in seminary based on his preaching).

However, I noticed that throughout the sermon, he gave the impression of feeling the same way about everything. Whether it was sharing something humorous, telling a sad story, or expositing a text, everything had the same emotional temperature. The following week, in our preaching cohort where (among other things) we evaluate messages, I shared that I felt he was disconnected emotionally from the content of his sermon. Others had picked up on it as well.

He graciously countered, saying that he felt incredibly engaged emotionally through the message. I replied that the problem wasn't a lack of emotional engagement, but that his engagement consisted of only one emotional level. Everything was treated with the same emotional weight. That's what news anchors or lecturers do, not preachers. If we could scale the emotional bandwidth of his sermon from one to ten, he spoke as if everything was a five.

- *Humorous anecdote – 5*
- *Sad story – 5*
- *Expositing Scripture – 5*
- *Call to Christ – 5*

When the emotional bandwidth of a sermon stays relatively close to stasis, it makes it seem to congregants like the preacher isn't moved by what he's speaking about. He's giving the impression of an observer, not a participant. For example, if your favorite football team scoring a touchdown provokes the same emotional response in you as asking for a hot dog at halftime, people would conclude you're either bored with the game or it doesn't really mean anything to you.[48]

Treating everything with the same emotional temperature moves our sermon into the bored factor. There's no dynamic to help the listener feel what you're saying. It's a betrayal of both your content and personality. Like the bull factor, this kind of preaching comes across as fake, because everyone has highs and lows they

---

[48] Or you're super crazy excited about hot dogs.

emotionally demonstrate in ways that befit their personality. Thus, if we get demonstrably excited or distressed in every other sphere of life except for the pulpit in which we preach, we're probably not preaching with our voice.

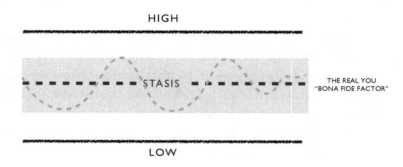

The goal is to preach in a way that naturally fills the highs and lows of one's emotional bandwidth zone. Don't overdo it (bull factor) or underdo it (bored factor). Preach within the real you, what I call the "bona fide factor." You're neither resorting to the cheap thrills of being melodramatic, nor hurting your content by being nonplussed in the preaching event. The bona fide sermon is one where you are emotionally yourself in the pulpit, naturally hitting the emotional notes that routinely evidence themselves in your personality. Remember that being you is what people connect with, what God uses, and where you want to be – the true you.

I suggest using others to help you better live into your emotional bandwidth because, more often than not, it's too difficult to discern by ourselves. Feedback is not just helpful, it is essential. Both of my illustrations involved someone outside the preacher identifying the emotional incongruence in the message. People who love and know us well can help us realize if, in our preaching, we're frequently moving into the bull factor or merely hovering around the bored factor, in the hopes we might make the corrections and find our way into the bona fide factor, where we find not only greater freedom in preaching but our voice as well.

WATCH YOURSELF

You can add yourself to the feedback loop by committing to watch your sermons on video. It's difficult to do and even painful, because we tend to be harder on ourselves in self-evaluation. Frankly, I've found myself slipping into bits of depression (using that term mildly) after watching a few of my sermons. But there are fewer things I have found as helpful in becoming a better preacher as watching myself preach. You need to see you.

Preachers tend to perceive themselves and their preaching in ways that don't hold to the reality everyone else in the pews is experiencing. Watching yourself preach helps you witness what you can't any other way. It will either confirm your thoughts about your preaching or contradict them. It's often a little bit of both. In skiing, coaches use video feedback so that athletes can see in real-time how they make turns, engage moguls, or accomplish the thousand other aspects to getting down a run. In preaching, video feedback may grant you a greater awareness about...

- How fast or slow you speak
- If your gestures are helpful or distracting
- If you maintain good or poor posture
- Whether your sermon had an emotional center or not

If you do embark on videoing yourself, it would be wise to remember an old baseball maxim: Don't get too high in your highs or get too low in your lows. In other words, don't turn in your two weeks notice if you see things in your preaching video that make you cringe, or sick to your stomach. The point of watching yourself is to grow as a preacher, to better find your voice and leverage it.

Take a chance. Commit to watch your preaching. Even after a couple of decades in the pulpit, I still try to watch my sermons on a weekly basis. I believe it's one of the best tools for my personal growth as a preacher.

TRUST YOUR CALLING

I want to finish this chapter encouraging you to embrace one last practice as you continue moving forward in your preaching ministry. Remember, finding your voice is about trusting that God chose you *as you* to preach – with all your personality quirks, level of intelligence, and emotional makeup. He chose you, not a version of someone else disguised as you. God didn't call me as John MacArthur, John Piper, Tim Keller, or whoever happens to be my favorite preacher at the moment (don't worry, yours will likely change over time too). He chose me, Yancey Arrington, to preach as Yancey Arrington. If God called you to preach, that means he called you to preach as you. Trust your calling!

Look how Paul introduced himself in his letters to the various churches he taught:

- "Paul, a servant of Christ Jesus, *called to be* an apostle, *set apart* for the gospel of God..." (Rom. 1:1)
- "Paul, *called by the will of God to be* an apostle of Christ Jesus..." (1 Cor. 1:1)
- "Paul, an apostle of Christ Jesus *by the will of God.*" (2 Cor. 1:1)
- "Paul, an apostle—*not from men nor through man, but through Jesus Christ and God the Father...*" (Gal. 1:1)
- "Paul, an apostle of Christ Jesus *by the will of God...*" (Eph. 1:1)
- "Paul, an apostle of Christ Jesus *by the will of God...*" (Col. 1:1)
- "Paul, an apostle of Christ Jesus *by command of God our Savior and of Christ Jesus our hope...*" (1 Tim. 1:1)
- "Paul, an apostle of Christ Jesus *by the will of God according to the promise of the life that is in Christ Jesus...*" (2 Tim. 1:1)

Ancient letters typically began with the author's name and, based on the kind of letter it was, a notation of credentials the author held in reference to the epistle's recipients. Paul wanted his congregations to know from the outset that his apostolic ministry was a calling from God. The Lord, in his good and perfect will, chose Paul to serve the church in a very specific capacity. Framing his letters with this introduction not only let these churches know where they stood with the apostle but also where the apostle stood with God: namely, that this specific ministry was the Lord's calling on his life.

Want to better find your voice in the pulpit? Lean on the fact God has called you (yes, you!) to preach his word. Your call likely wasn't as dramatic as Paul's on the Damascus road, but it is still a call from the same sovereign Lord. Let me offer a practice that might help you for a season, especially if you struggle with preaching like someone else in the pulpit. Consider writing at the top of your sermon notes a similar preface to Paul's[49]:

Colin Crawford
[Your name], a preacher of Jesus Christ
by the will of God.

Read this statement aloud to yourself every time you're in the study. Say this to yourself in the moments you feel tempted to be someone else in the pulpit. Whisper this to your heart right before you open up the Word of God to preach on Sunday. Because sometimes, the person who most needs to be reminded that God called you to preach *as* you *is* you!

Honestly, there have been seasons where I was so disappointed in the quality of my preaching ministry that I felt the only support I had to lean on was my calling as a preacher. It held me fast in seasons of strong doubts about my ability to preach. Yet, even in the middle of very dry times in the pulpit, I knew beyond a shadow of a doubt that God, as he had called Paul as an apostle, had also called me as a pastor with the ministry of preaching his Word. If I couldn't rest in anything else, I could at least rest in that.

Reminding my own heart that I was called to be a preacher by the will of God not only helped me understand where I stood in ministry, but where I stood with the Lord. The truth is, even after

---

[49] If you're a Millennial, consider tattooing it on the inside of your forearm (I kid, I kid).

multiple decades of preaching, there are seasons in the pulpit where these words are the very ones my heart still needs to hear. Maybe yours does too. Finding your voice rests on trusting your calling.

LET YOU BE YOU

As I've written, I share the pulpit with another pastor, our founding and senior pastor Bruce Wesley. Bruce brought me on staff as the Teaching Pastor when I was 26 and the church only four years old. A lot of leaders might consider that a gutsy move on Bruce's part, because many church planters are concerned with establishing themselves as the head honcho amongst their new congregation. That means, among other things, keeping the keys to the pulpit. Fortunately for me, Bruce was secure enough in both his leadership and teaching to let me have a seat at the preaching table from the moment I arrived in Houston.

In my first decade at Clear Creek, I regularly found myself being blown away by Bruce's preaching. I was confronted each week with sermons that were well-structured and insightful, with language crafted to perfection. I often would think to myself, "Man, I need to preach more like Bruce preaches." But in trying to preach Bruce's way, I implemented practices, approaches, and styles that not only were hard for me to do, but actually worked against the strengths of who I was in the pulpit. After experiencing enough frustration down this road, I finally came to grips with the fact that I wasn't Bruce. I was me. Better yet, God was responsible for my unique wiring. I either needed to accept that or get used to walking the road of disappointment and disillusionment in preaching.

One of my close preacher friends recently took a sabbatical, some of which he spent in counseling. When I asked how it went, he said that he grew immensely in areas such as self-awareness and how his family of origin shaped much of his personality. I then asked how this had impacted his ministry since his return from the sabbatical. Without hesitation he answered, "Yancey, I'm preaching better than I've ever preached before." The point was that the better he knew himself, the better he preached.

While it's taken me longer than I'd like to admit, I hope these steps can help shorten your window to finding your voice. Make sure when you alight upon the pulpit each Sunday to open up the oracles of God, it's you who is preaching.

Finding your voice is ultimately about getting comfortable with yourself because you can't be anyone else. Ski the way you need to ski. Get down the mountain in the way that fits you best! If we're trying to be someone else in the pulpit, we are ultimately robbing God, his church, and ourselves. God made you to be you with all your strengths and weaknesses. I may get down the mountain of my messages differently than others who I admire, but when I've reached the bottom and see that my congregation has been along for the ride, I take great joy in knowing that God used me *as me* to do it. May he do the same for you as you get down the mountain!

CONCLUSION

"And my speech and my message were not in plausible
words of wisdom, but in demonstration of the Spirit
and of power, so that your faith might not rest
in the wisdom of men, but in the power of God."
— I CORINTHIANS 2:4-5

Preaching may be easy for some, but it hasn't been for me, especially early in my ministry. There have been days when disappointment got the best of me. I've even considered leaving the pulpit altogether. You see, there is a broken part of me tied to performance and merit-based living that whispers in my ear, "Yancey, if this is the best sermon you can muster then you need a new seat on the staff bus." Granted, I don't hear that voice as often as I've grown in understanding my gospel identity. But those doubts dogged me long enough to cause me to look upon my pulpit ministry with great caution and reservation.

Some of my issues flow from the fact that my preaching is a much more intuitive than systematic process. I'm frequently asked about how I put messages together. I'm embarrassed to reply because of my inability to share point-by-point how it happens. It looks different almost every time I do it. Sometimes I start breaking down a text on paper, or I brainstorm the flow of an idea on a marker board, or I research for a period of time and then write the sermon from start to finish. In my 20-year tenure as the Teaching Pastor at Clear Creek Community Church, I've preached over 800 sermons. One would think I'd have an established message preparation process by now, but I don't. That's nuts! Frankly, it bothers me that it's the case.

However, this angst in my preaching is completely internal. There is not a week which goes by where I don't have several encouraging, uplifting emails filling my inbox about how God has used my latest message in the lives of my parishioners. I am very, very grateful for that. Furthermore, I'm part of a leadership staff which reinforces my teaching gift with similar votes of confidence and support. That's a big deal to me as well. I tend to give a louder voice in my life to those whom I deeply respect, and there are few men I respect as much as those who comprise Clear Creek Community Church's executive staff. Make no mistake, my struggle with preaching is one where I'm in a room locked from the inside. Maybe you know what that room looks like, too.

This book is my humble attempt to share the way I think about preaching. I was bothered that I couldn't explain to others what came intuitively to me in the pulpit. So, when I began to help those on my staff with their preaching, I started thinking of ways to communicate what I believed was critical to preaching. These were concepts I knew wouldn't be found in a seminary classroom or books on homiletics.

Things like feeling through a sermon, charting its bandwidth, and looking for the emotional center of a message were concepts and phrases I created because: 1) I needed some kind of language to communicate to my fellow staffers, and 2) I couldn't find those concepts in any resources (although I'm quite certain that is due to my inadequacy in finding them, not their nonexistence). What you see in this book are the fruits of that labor, which I've been encouraged by my church's leadership and other preachers to share with you.

It's taken a bit of time to write this book because, well, I have a church to pastor. There are sermons to prepare and preach, people to lead, and a myriad of other assignments my role demands as many of you pastors well know. My focus and calling is to the local church. She's the priority for my ministry. It's also the reason I hope you give these ideas about preaching a real chance. They aren't born in the ivory tower of philosophical ideas, but from the better part of two decades of not only preaching that has moved people but also helping others to effectively do the same. You can preach to move people, too. Yes, there is work to be done in the message and the messenger – both in the *how* and the *who* – but it's a work that will last a lifetime in the pulpit. Each year can be sweeter than the next. Each Sunday can be the exhilarating experience of taking your listeners down the mountain of your message, not only showing them the majesty and wonder of the gospel of Christ but compelling them to return again and again for another journey. There's only one question left to ask: *Are you ready to put on your skis?*

About The Author

Since 1998, Dr. Yancey Arrington has served as the Teaching Pastor at Clear Creek Community Church, a multi-campus congregation of around 5,000 in the Bay Area of Houston. He is passionate about, and coaches others on, gospel-centrality, preaching, theology, leadership, and church planting.

A native Texan, Yancey loves to spend time with family and friends at his family's ranch house in the Texas Hill Country. He is also an avid sports fan with a soft spot in his heart for the Baylor Bears and Houston Astros.

Yancey holds a BA in Religion from Baylor University, a Masters of Divinity with Biblical Languages from Southwestern Seminary, and a Doctor of Ministry from Covenant Seminary. He is husband to Jennefer and father to three boys: Thatcher, Haddon, and Beckett.

You can read more from Yancey at
YanceyArrington.com

or follow him on Twitter
@YanceyArrington

ALSO FROM YANCEY ARRINGTON

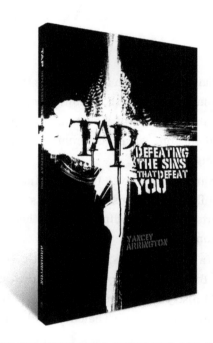

COULD IT BE THE REASON THAT SIN OFTEN WINS IS BECAUSE YOU BEGAN WITH THE WRONG STRATEGY?

Some have been defeated by certain sins for so long it seems hopeless. We do our best to fight by reading the Bible, praying, and engaging in other spiritual disciplines, yet still find ourselves down on the mat more than we care to admit. In *TAP: Defeating the Sins that Defeat You*, author and teacher Yancey Arrington looks to some of history's best sin-fighters, John Owen and the Puritans, to find out why the "Just Do More" approach to the spiritual disciplines may be the wrong strategy to defeating sin. *TAP* exposes some of the more popular, but ultimately inept approaches and beliefs about sin, repentance, and spiritual growth while coaching how to get "into the cage" with our sins and not only survive...but win! Discussion questions included with each chapter.

CPSIA information can be obtained
at www.ICGtesting.com
Printed in the USA
BVHW060049041118
531461BV00002B/7/P